The Thrift Book

LIVE WELL AND SPEND LESS

India Knight

PENGUIN BOOKS

PENGUIN BOOKS

Published by the Penguin Group
Penguin Books Ltd, 80 Strand, London WC2R 0RL, England
Penguin Group (USA) Inc., 375 Hudson Street, New York, New York 10014, USA
Penguin Group (Canada), 90 Eglinton Avenue East, Suite 700, Toronto, Ontario, Canada M4P 2Y3
(a division of Pearson Penguin Canada Inc.)
Penguin Ireland, 25 St Stephen's Green, Dublin 2, Ireland (a division of Penguin Books Ltd)
Penguin Group (Australia), 250 Camberwell Road,
Camberwell, Victoria 3124, Australia (a division of Pearson Australia Group Pty Ltd)
Penguin Books India Pvt Ltd, 11 Community Centre,
Panchsheel Park, New Delhi – 110 017, India
Penguin Group (NZ), 67 Apollo Drive, Rosedale, North Shore 0632, New Zealand
(a division of Pearson New Zealand Ltd)
Penguin Books (South Africa) (Pty) Ltd, 24 Sturdee Avenue,
Rosebank, Johannesburg 2196, South Africa

Penguin Books Ltd, Registered Offices: 80 Strand, London WC2R 0RL, England

www.penguin.com

First published by Fig Tree 2008
Published in Penguin Books 2009
4

Copyright © India Knight, 2008
Illustrations copyright © Debbie Powell, 2008

The moral right of the author and of the illustrator has been asserted

Set in Filosofia and Ingrid Darling
Printed in Great Britain by Clays Ltd, St Ives plc

A CIP catalogue record for this book is available from the British Library

ISBN: 978-0-141-03823-0

Contents

Thanks to Andrew, whose prescient idea this book originally was, and who once tried, thriftily but unsuccessfully, to get my children to play with peg dolls ('See they wee pegs? That's all youse need tae play fer ooers. Hey! Come back! Och, youse are spoilt wee bastards, just like yer maw'). Huge special thanks to lovely Sophia for feeding and clothing said children while I typed, and for providing them with better play materials. Giant thanks also to Laura Wheatley for being an ace researcher; to the unbeatable combo of Georgia Garrett and Juliet Annan for everything; and to Jenny Lord for her help, insight and dazzling efficiency. And thank you to Sarah Fraser for this beautiful design, and to Debbie Powell for her wonderful illustrations.

Introduction

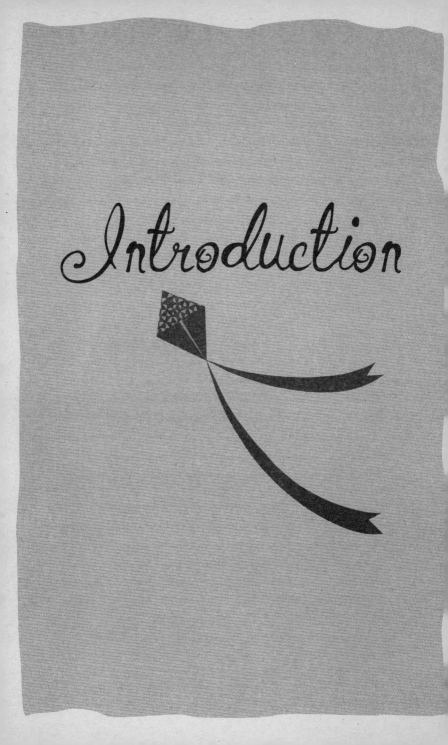

$\mathcal{T}$o say I've never found the idea of 'cutting back' particularly appealing would be something of an understatement. I am naturally extravagant; I am also naturally spectacularly crap with money, regardless of how much or how little of it I earn. It's an unhappy combination that has, for two decades, resulted in complete dependency on my overdraft facility and on assorted loans, and in long periods of a panic-denial-panic cycle. Let's just say I've come across my fair share of bailiffs over the years (one year they appeared on 23 December, which was nice. I was out shopping). When it comes to money, I am Fiddling While Rome Burns made flesh. Or rather, I was.

In 2007, before I decided that I really needed to get a grip once and for all, I was served with bankruptcy papers – not for the first time, but for the most inescapable, disastrous one. I had two books in the Top Ten bestseller charts at the time. It's not that I can't earn money, or that I don't earn enough of it. It's a complete inability to manage money, full stop – and, to be frank, an inborn lack of interest in doing so: money, schmoney; sometimes you have it, sometimes you don't – whatever (it's perhaps no coincidence that my father died a double bankrupt and that my mother's attitude to money is, shall we say, quite breezy). This romantic and deluded view works fine(ish) if there's just one of you, but it has rather limited appeal if you have a family – children to clothe, food to put on the table, bills to pay because if you don't the baby gets hypothermia, that kind of thing.

I'll get back to all of this in the relevant chapter, but I think, embarrassingly enough, that, genetics aside, my calamitous approach to finances stems from some bizarre notion that I was too 'creative', too 'carefree' (ha!) to concern myself with the rather naffly bourgeois issue of money management. Just as I used to see being fat as being indicative of having a wonderful appetite for life (as well as buns), I think I subconsciously saw my financial idiocy as a sign of a rather charmingly bohemian easy-come-easy-go approach to life in general. I know: it's pathetic.

Also, I am forty-two years old. I've got over lying in the bath pretending to be Ophelia, but, clearly, not over thinking money is, like, really, really square.

I share all of this rather intimate information to pre-empt the obvious accusation about my writing this book: i.e. that it's all very well for a well-paid, relatively successful middle-class person who lives in a lovely house in a lovely corner of London to write about thrift – pull the other one, Marie Antoinette, it's got a Sèvres cowbell on. But actually, my investigations into – and eventual embracing of – thrift have their roots in necessity. It dawned on me that nothing was going to improve unless I made fundamental changes to my spending habits. You may not have been served with sinister legal papers or become blasé about bailiffs, but it's a rare bird these days that doesn't feel a little belt-tightening might be in order, what with recession, mortgage rates, the credit crunch, the rise in the cost of living, and the disconcerting feeling that your profession and income ought to result in a rather more comfortable, less stressful lifestyle than your current one.

Walking-money-disaster aside, my new-found love of thrift also has its roots in a strange and unfamiliar feeling that has been creeping up on me incrementally over the past few years. I am a child of the 1980s: I believe in consumption, conspicuous or furtive. I love shopping so much that I wrote a whole book about it.* I have no guilt about the number of handbags I own. Many of my generation despised 'hippies', and by extension despised 'hippieish' habits such as recycling, or reusing wrapping paper, or buggering about making compost, or wearing second-hand clothes, or knitting your own socks – hey,

* The Shops, *published by Penguin. Go on, line my pocket.*

why not macramé your armpit hair while you're at it, loser? We were
(much too) proud of our cash and of the things it could buy, even if, in
retrospect, our attitude smacked rather embarrassingly of defensiveness
and disengagement: well, I earn more than you, so that must make me
better than you, right? (Wrong, wrong, wrong, and incredibly twattish
to boot, though much of my generation couldn't see it at the time.)

But anyway, hippie-contempt aside, as the years passed even I succumbed
to imperceptible greening – my older children, by the way, were miles
ahead of me on this one, and my four-year-old sips her carton of juice and
then sticks it in the recycling bag without being asked. I started finding

myself peculiarly irritated at the amount of plastic used in supermarket packaging. You know the kind of thing: you want apples, but the apples come in their own pre-moulded plastic tray, with a layer of pre-moulded plastic foam to protect them from 'bruising', as though the journey home involved riding bareback through the Kalahari. Then I got a bit of a bee in my bonnet about plastic bags, because I kept seeing them depressingly out of context: on beaches, in trees, in the sky, on water. And because I read all the papers every day for my job, then I thought that it was really pretty shameful and just plain *ugly* to be shoving said papers, several trees' worth, into a bin liner every week.

I started noticing that we chucked a lot of food away as well, and I didn't like it. I knew the starving children of the world wouldn't starve any less because I was binning sprouty potatoes or stale bread, but the binning didn't make me feel good. With no famine on the horizon and shops within walking distance, why was I buying too much food week after week? And so on. Little by little, I became greener. We're talking eau de Nil, or chartreuse on a good day, rather than darkest forest green, but there was a perceptible shift in my attitudes to things I'd taken for granted for years. I began to mind about waste. The question of waste didn't keep me up at night, but it lodged itself in my consciousness and made itself at home. Today, I can't imagine not recycling – it's just what you do; and I can't imagine merrily chucking away perfectly good food either. Or being mean about hippies. And it's interesting to note that they have turned from being easy-to-ridicule figures of hilarity – grubby-looking, with Peruvian knitwear – to rather admirable conscience-prickers and, well, pioneers.

At the same time as all of this, I began to find my own conspicuous consumption slightly nauseating. Not all the time, obviously: I understand, and dearly love, the thrilling kick of pure pleasure that comes from buying a lovely dress, or indeed a lovely holiday, and I'm not into self-flagellation (or into wearing hideous clothes, no matter how worthy). But there was, it slowly dawned on me, something really rather gross about wanting something and buying it, just like that – thank you, Amex, and sod the consequences. I'm not talking about buying hairgrips or Tampax, but rather about spending two or three figures on something that I didn't remotely need, on the basis that it made me happy and therefore why not?

Now, I know I am EXTREMELY FORTUNATE to be able to have done this at all, and I know most people don't just wander into Selfridges and think, hmm, what to spend my hard-earned cash on today? And I know I sound spoilt, but I'm trying to be honest. Besides, the Selfridges scenario plays itself out nationally every Saturday afternoon and during many a weekday lunch hour. The amounts of money may be smaller, the destination may be the local high street, but the instinct is the same. It says, 'Let's go shopping': i.e. 'Let's buy random stuff we don't actually need.' Five years ago, buying stuff I didn't need was my idea of bliss. I liked the process and I liked being the kind of person who is able to buy themselves (and their friends and family) presents. I still like presents, but these days my treat of choice comes from a yarn shop in north London, not from the Chloé concession in Selfridges, and if I want to give someone I really care about a present, I may actually – gasp! – make them something. And here's the clincher: I would consider the something as chic and stylish as anything a department store could have produced. Chicer, sometimes.

That's another thing that has changed with the passing of time. If someone adult had given you a home-made gift a few years ago, you'd have thought, aah, bless, and shoved it in a drawer. If someone gave you one this afternoon, you'd be delighted. One of my favourite recent birthday presents was a beautifully knitted lurex scarf. Not only had the friend who made it gone to the trouble of sitting there knitting for me, but she'd had some little Cash's name tapes made that said 'Made for you with love by Alison' in red curly writing. The woman's a lawyer; she doesn't have much spare time. Her partner appeared at my house with a cake he'd baked and

lugged across half of London. They could have gone anywhere and spent any amount on my present, but it wouldn't have made me feel a fraction as delighted.

So: feeling poorer, feeling greener, minding more, realizing that you don't have to be a professional to be able to make things with your hands and that making things with your hands is unexpectedly and wonderfully rewarding. There's another component to the thrift U-turn and it is to do with snobbery of, I fear, a very middle-class kind. (Actually I don't fear *at all* – I'm so over having to apologize for being middle class.) It is this: if, as is apparently and slightly mysteriously the case, half the world and his neighbour are holidaying in Barbados and toting huge Marc Jacobs bags around while flicking their expensive caramel highlights, the currency of such goods becomes, to our eyes, devalued – which is just as well, as we can't afford them any more anyway. Things aren't as desirable if everyone has them. What's good for democracy is bad for uniqueness, for feeling that what you have is special and worth cherishing. Democracy also vulgarizes: things become common in both senses. Individualism is the loser.

Call me an atrocious human being, but I don't want to be like everybody else. I really mind about the things I surround myself with and I want to feel that they are special, significant and meaningful. What I'm describing is, if you will, the difference between dining off bangers and mash on prettily mismatched plates, in an unfitted and individualistic kitchen with a pot of rosemary on the table, and dining off foie gras on Wedgwood in a 'designer' apartment which has gold taps in the bathrooms and orchids by each place card. For some of us, everything's gone a bit gold taps, a bit orchid. What we'd like is some authenticity, some individualism, some soul in our lives. I can't believe I'm going to use this word (I shall go and macramé my 'pits in a minute), but: some integrity. Less surface, more content. Less doing-it-by-numbers, more originality. Fewer shallows, greater depths.

Enter thrift, or at least a manageable, workaday version of it. The greatest surprise to me while living my new thrifty life is how much fun it is. Well, actually no. The greatest surprise is the amazing amount of money it's saving me a month: it seems almost incredible. The second greatest surprise is the fun. The third, unexpectedly, is the genuine pleasure I find in making do and mending, in being creative, in thinking about little things properly, in affording small domestic concerns the same attention as I afford *Newsnight* – in a real and useful way, not in a 'Let's Play Ironic Retro Housewife' way (though when the Doris Day moment strikes, as it occasionally does, I like it very much).

And the fourth surprise, no less important, is the sense, long lost and now regained, that I am doing my bit. I understand that my bit is very small and that, globally, one First World person's idea of thrift is another Third World person's idea of unimaginable, obscene luxury. But we all do what we can and it's got to be better than doing nothing at all. I'll never be a full-on eco-warrior, or become a fan of those hideous light bulbs we're all supposed to switch to even though they make everything look disgustingly ugly, and I'll always choose indulgence over sanctity. Give me a farm, a private income and some staff and I'd be delighted to be greener-than-thou and fully organic (marry me off to Louis XVI while you're at it, or maybe Sting), but the reality is I'm a single mother of three with serious demands on my time, and if that sometimes means spaghetti hoops on white toast or half an hour's peace courtesy of PlayStation, or plastic toys rather than artisanal wooden ones, so be it. This is not a guide called *How to Be Green*, or *How to Be Good* (and nor is it a guide called *How to Be Mean*. I despise meanness. If you want to learn to be mean, stop reading and go away – you're banned). If you want to read about the kind of thrift that involves saving rubber bands, bundling them up and turning them into balls to give your children for Christmas, or if the idea of spending two hours filling in forms to get 50p off something appeals, or if you're a fan of coupons, this is not the right book for you. It's not about cheese-paring. It's about living well, for less.

But if you're interested in living well and stylishly, in valuing beauty, in saving money in unexpectedly satisfying ways and in feeling like a useful member of the human race at the same time as enhancing your life in dozens of little but significantly pleasing ways, read on. You have nothing to lose but your overdraft – and nothing to gain but a fresh look at the true value of things, yourself included. This is why, even if Euro Millions chose me to be the lone and especial beneficiary of its largesse, I'd still think twice about dumping the lifestyle changes described in these pages. Being thrifty makes you feel good about yourself, and you can't put a price on that.

Food

This seems the obvious place to start. We all have to eat and I can't be the only person to have done a normal-seeming supermarket shop and literally dropped my jaw at the bill. Worse, you do the huge supermarket shop, have a funny turn at the total, donkey the bags back home, unpack a pile of stuff – and find that, once you've taken out the dishwasher tablets and the laundry detergent and the loo paper, it only really fills two shelves of the fridge and might last you three days tops. How did that happen? And how did we get to the stage where, shamefully, a couple of the perishable things bought on Monday end up in the bin by Friday?

Sensible Supermarket Shopping and How to Do It

Don't. Shop locally, daily, buying only precisely what you need: a bag of pasta, say, and some overripe tomatoes going cheap at the grocer's. Add an onion, olive oil and some basil from your windowsill and you have supper for four for about 50p a head.* This works extremely well on the thriftiness front, but I do see it can also be completely and irritatingly unpractical for most people who work. In which case . . .

* *All costings worked out using prices on www.mysupermarket.co.uk.*

Shop online. This is soothing and unstressful, and you can do it while keeping an eye on the telly, sipping a glass of wine. It also discourages that kind of weird, slightly dazed aisle-browsing most of us do – 'Oh, a wonderful new delicious-looking product. I'll just stick some in my trolley, even though I have no idea when we'll eat it, or what with' – as well as discouraging the loony impulse buy, as in, 'Wow! Towels! So cheap and yet so fluffy! Must buy some!' even though it's hardly as if your whole family stands about drip-drying after every bath. When I am at the supermarket and not in a tearing hurry, I often become temporarily insane, buying things simply because I'm pleased to find Sainsbury's (or whoever) stocks them. Wow, harissa. Wow, avocado oil. Wow, other ludicrously expensive stuff that sits on the shelves gathering dust and never being used, since my home life is not the home life sold to me by lifestyle magazines ('What shall I do with my spare hour? I know. I'll make a tagine. In fact, I'll make an entire Moroccan-themed supper, just for the fun of it.' I mean, please). I am also prone to moments of madness in the bathroom aisles. I have perfectly good shampoo at home, but am lured by the idea that this one might be better. I have bought soap I don't need because of its packaging (Waitrose, at the time of writing, sells a perfectly ordinary bar of soap for £6. Six quid! For a bar of soap!). Avoiding the supermarket is not only much easier on the pocket, but easier on the sanity.

Better still, shop online from a properly compiled list. What I now do is sit down with my recipe books and plan out what I'm going to be cooking that week – yes, I know, I am a good little housewife. I don't apologize for it: it is intensely satisfying – check my shelves and fridge, and write down a list of missing ingredients. Not only does this save you a fortune – no impulse buys, nothing unnecessary, nothing you can't use, nothing that's going to sit there quietly going past its sell-by date* – but it stops you buying snacky things that make you fat. Granted, it's more time-consuming, but it saves you a packet.

Make that properly compiled list as ingenious as you can and a tribute to the lost art of good housekeeping, where the leftovers from Sunday lunch made at least two extra meals. If, say, you're going to roast a chicken, find an onion, a stick of celery and a couple of carrots so you can make chicken stock and then soup. Or get some lettuce (home-grown, ideally, ergo free, see pages 31–2) and Parmesan to make a chicken Caesar out of the leftovers, or really good bread (home-made is cheaper; there are thousands of recipes online) for chicken sandwiches the next day. Speaking of chicken, here's a tip: I always want to make chicken stock, but don't necessarily have the time or inclination as soon as supper is finished, so what I do now is chuck the whole carcass in the freezer, where it will live quite happily for several weeks. I either make my stock (which gives me soup and the base for delicious risottos, among other things) a few days later, or wait until there are two or three carcasses, which will give a wonderfully concentrated, rich stock and make the house smell really cosy on a wintry afternoon – cheaper than candles and nicer to come home to when it's pelting down outside.

If you physically go to the supermarket, do a tiny bit of detective work and find out at what time of day they start discounting things. This will vary from store to store but is usually in the early evening: i.e. at an ideal time if you're coming home from work. A friend of mine literally follows the bloke with the pricing gun and then makes herself feasts out of the random things she's bought, pretending she's on *Ready Steady Cook*. If you are the *Ready Steady Cook* type and are

---

* *I cannot responsibly suggest you ignore sell-by dates, but I would nevertheless urge you to use your common sense. Nothing terrible is going to happen to a yogurt that's a couple of days overdue; though the same wouldn't necessarily be true of a piece of raw chicken.*

inspired by making that evening's meal out of random purchases, then obviously the injunction on page 16 to shop from a list may not apply.

If you find yourself naturally resistant to the idea of buying discounted food because you're middle class, get over it. It was £5 thirty seconds ago and now it's £2.50. It's exactly the same food. Nothing has happened to it. Snap it up and count your blessings. Besides, it's really very naff and petit bourgeois to mind about this kind of thing. Nobody loves a bargain as much as posh people do – the ones I know are spectacularly mean, which must be part of the reason they're rich in the first place. If you're troubled by dented tins, pretend you're a member of the landed gentry. This also applies if you're bothered by having to wear frayed shirts, Harry Potter hair or jumbo cords from 1976. You're in grand company.

All supermarkets put the most expensive stuff at eye level. Look up or down for the perfectly respectable, cheaper options.

Stop shopping at the 'posh' supermarkets. They're insanely overpriced. I've shaved a fortune off my monthly food bill by frequenting my local non-posh supermarkets, which I'd previously discounted on the snobby basis that they felt like shopping in Albania in 1971 – semi-bare shelves, hideous lighting. I've got over it. I don't see why I should pay a grotesque premium just because the veg is stored in pretty baskets rather than on workaday plastic shelving. Lidl is remarkably cheap and, being German, sells really good ham, salami, sausages and other meat products, and also fantastic dark chocolate. I've tried noticing what the difference is taste-wise between a Lidl avocado and an M&S one, but I can't. And I'm picky. So dump your prejudices at the door and save a whole load. To give you a rough idea: at the time of writing, a box of Fruit 'n Fibre cereal cost £2.17 at Waitrose and 89p at Lidl. It's the same product! A pineapple cost £1.49 at Waitrose and 49p at Lidl. A pineapple is a pineapple. And so on. There's no point in being snooty. The only person who ends up being a mug is you. There is a whole world of information about this on the thrifty person's number-one website, www.moneysavingexpert.com, specifically here: www.moneysavingexpert.com/shopping/are-cheap-supermarkets-good.

If you insist on frequenting the posh supermarkets for your organic raw meat (for instance) that's one thing, but you'd have to be a fool to buy your dishwasher tablets from them too. Or loo paper, or detergent, or dry goods – you're paying a vast premium for no reason whatsoever.

Beware of the bargain that isn't, as per the cheap towels above. A bargain is only a bargain if it's something you actually need. If it is merely cheap, you're still spending money on something unnecessary, which is not a bargain at all but a pointless and depressing waste of money. (This also applies, with knobs on, to shopping for clothes in the sales – see page 72.)

Don't be snobby about what you will and won't buy from the supermarket. Waitrose, for instance, does a really delicious organic chicken (Sheepdrove Organic Chicken, it's called)

which, at the time of writing, is £4 cheaper than the significantly less delicious chicken from my award-winning fancy-pants organic butcher's. I absolutely support this butcher's, and small local shops in general, and there is a part of me that believes supermarkets are really quite evil (though not Waitrose – it's part of the John Lewis group, which operates, laudably, as a cooperative, which means it's held in trust on behalf of all its employees, who have a say in how the business is run and receive a share of the annual profits). But there is also a certain kind of mimsy foodie preciousness that brings me out in hives. In an ideal world we'd all have access to a lovely local baker's and butcher's and fishmonger's, and these would all be competitively priced, but most of us don't live in such a world. We don't have time to arse around sniffing special loaves of bread made by the thrillingly gnarled fingers of French peasants – or to pay a premium for them. Most of us work and have families, most of us are both time- and cash-strapped, ergo most of us use supermarkets. The trick is to use them intelligently rather than mindlessly.

The excellent www.mysupermarket.co.uk works like an ordinary online supermarket. You fill your trolley with stuff, but, brilliantly, it then works out whether you'd be better off shopping at Tesco, Sainsbury's, Ocado (Waitrose) or Asda, based on what you're buying. The differences can be startling and it gives you further ways to cut your bill as you reach the checkout. The site is updated daily with the latest offers. You can then buy online and book a delivery with any of them apart from Asda, who don't deliver (but you can print out your shopping list from the site and take it there in person, which is better than nothing).

You can compare and review own-brand products from Aldi, Lidl, Co-op and Asda at www.supermarketownbrandguide.co.uk. It is often (but not always) the case that own-brand products are essentially the same as branded ones: X company, for instance, makes its own line of posh chocolates, but also produces only marginally less posh ones for Y supermarket. Own-brand products aren't in the premium/Finest/ultra-organic league, but when you're talking about a can of tomatoes, that isn't necessarily a disaster – or even a problem.

We all, I think, have particular anxieties about food and thriftiness. In our heads, it's tied up with economy mince and a depressing sort of joylessness – we don't like to think of ourselves as economy-mince kinds of guys. Who does? I make no apology for the fact that I eat only organic meat and eggs, and usually (but by no means always) buy organic veg too. I can't countenance feeding myself or my children intensively farmed junk-meat; I'd rather just be vegetarian.* I

don't do convenience food either. Not only are ready-meals nutritionally deplorable and full of dubious, fattening, bloat-causing, mood-altering crap, but they are *unbelievably* expensive compared to something fresh cooked from scratch † (talk about a giant con – they're bad for you and expensive. Where's the 'convenience'?). Having said that, I don't eat meat every day – or even every week – and I buy judicious cuts: see pages 40–41.

* *A carnivore writes: we should, really, all become vegetarian. This isn't the time or the place to give a lecture about forests being destroyed to make way for grazing cattle, or the effect this has on climate change – a 2006 United Nations report found that cattle-rearing generated more greenhouse gases than transportation – but anyone who is even slightly concerned about the shape of the planet, or its future, might want to read up on this.*

† *At the time of writing, one pot of ready-made fancy-pants mash (who buys this stuff?) costs the same as 10lb of potatoes. Seriously.*

This isn't a book about being on the breadline. But there is, we need to realize, a middle path between those Value tins and going mad at the deli counter with the Parma ham. Not that there's anything wrong with some of those Value tins (or with tins in general, actually). Some contain undelicious, unfanciable things, but if you need chopped tomatoes to make a sauce, frankly the Value tomatoes aren't going to ruin your recipe: ditto baked beans, ditto canned salmon. It doesn't do to be too precious, either financially or as a human being.

We're told time and time again by fashionable television chefs that cooking is all about the spanking wonderfulness of our top-quality, ultra-premium ingredients. This is true up to a point, but not nearly as true as they'd have you believe. Feeding yourself well is also about being a good enough cook to transform base into gold. There is nothing intrinsically impressive about a £15 super-chicken being an amazing thing to eat; I'm rather more impressed by someone doing something marvellous with the free-range chicken thighs that were on special offer.

The post-war generation may have been used to never throwing a single scrap away, and, my older friends tell me, to making endless amounts of stuffed pancakes and rissoles, and eking out Sunday's roast for a good four days beyond, but those of us who have had the luxury of always living in relatively affluent times can feel quite panicky at the idea of stretching things out, or of feeding four people for a fiver. It's going to be grotty, we think. It's going to taste cheap, or look cheap, and makes us look as if we live like students. If we're attempting to feed friends rather than partners and children, that anxiety gets ratcheted up a notch: feeding people is, after all, about generosity and largesse, about providing for loved ones. None of these qualities really go with cutting corners, we think.

I wouldn't be so sure. Some of my happiest suppers have centred around the baked potato and rough red wine model, and my natural preference is still for a slightly ponced-up version of the same: really delicious macaroni cheese and home-grown salad, say, rather than anything that smacks overly of the old Cordon Bleu, or that is presented in stacks, or that comes with its own jus. The British have such odd attitudes to food, or perhaps just such recent attitudes to food. It doesn't seem an especially wild generalization to say nobody cared at all until about 1950 and the advent of Elizabeth David (granted, they'd had a couple of world wars, plus their aftermaths, to contend with. But the disastrous culinary aftermath doesn't seem to have applied to the French, or the Belgians, or the Italians, or the Spanish, so one is forced to conclude that the British just didn't mind that much about what they put in their mouths).

This nervousness is particularly manifest in relation to 'entertaining'. For some reason, a surprising number of people still feel that a 'dinner party' is preferable to a kitchen supper and requires, to be successful, linen napkins, stiff little flower arrangements and expensive ingredients, to say nothing of giant amounts of effort. Actually, what it requires is excellent company, the kind of friendly food everyone likes to eat and copious amounts of wine and water – tap, please: it's free and it tastes good. Bottled water has had its day, in terms of both the money it costs and the plastic it uses (plus, not to be alarmist or anything, but you might want to Google 'plastic water bottle + antimony'). If you're really worried about drinking tap, install an under-the-counter filter – it'll pay for itself in a few weeks and you won't contribute to landfill. Try www.freshwaterfilter.com. If you're concerned, as some are, about chemicals from plastic filters leaching into the water supply, try a ceramic version, as used by the International Red Cross: www.naturalcollection. com/natural-products/pure-water-in-natural-terracotta.aspx.

The evenings we remember aren't the ones where the meal was Michelin-standard but rather the ones where the food was cosy and comfortable and everyone laughed a lot. So the first thing to do is to relax and stop approaching the question of what to feed other people as though it were a military campaign, or a personality test that would reveal all sorts of deep secrets about you, one of which being that you're cheap. Nobody cares, or if they do you need to get yourself some new friends. And if Michelin-standard cooking is your thing, you needn't feel crippled by a lack of expensive ingredients. *Au contraire*, aside from anything else, it's what *cuisine du terroir* is all about, with its dependence on local ingredients and peasant traditions.

The notion of thrifty food sounds so mean and pinched, but the fact of the matter is that being thrifty does not have to mean an end to abundance, merely an end to waste and excess. And when I say waste and excess, I mean waste and excess – a THIRD of all the food we buy goes to waste. This is not good for the environment, obviously, since all the energy that goes into producing, transporting, packaging and storing the food is also wasted, and it is really not good for the pocket either. Or, frankly, for morale. There is a brilliant website, www.lovefoodhatewaste.com, that concerns itself with all of this, and with finding really ingenious solutions. It has, among a whole slew of other things, tips on getting portion sizes right and on the best way of keeping, freezing and using up leftovers, and provides you with free recipes that centre around using up stray vegetables and other bits and bobs that might otherwise be headed for the bin. Just select the ingredient you have left over, be it potatoes, carrots or cheese, etc., and up pop any number of suitable recipes. Genius.

I must detour at this point and recommend two wonderful books. The first is an absolutely brilliant little volume by Gill Holcombe, a mother of three, called (deep breath) *How to Feed Your Whole Family a Healthy Balanced Diet with Very Little Money and Hardly Any Time Even If You Have* a Tiny Kitchen, Only Three Saucepans (One with an Ill-fitting Lid) and No Fancy Gadgets – Unless You Count the Garlic Crusher. It costs £9.99 and is published by Spring Hill Books. The hearty, honest, family-friendly recipes are delicious and she means it about 'very little money' – the weekly meal planners at the back of the book include shopping lists with costings (for 2007) and average out at about £30 a week for a family of four (and she only uses organic meat. QED). I can't recommend this book highly enough.

The second book you may want to look at is, maddeningly, £25 – do have a browse before you buy, or ask for it for a present, though to be fair it is practically encyclopedia-sized. But it's also a marvel in its way. Called *The Kitchen Revolution* (Ebury), its premise is to return to the days of good housekeeping, save money, time and effort, and put an end to waste. The premise is achieved. This is a foodier book than the previous one, but not poncily so. It is quite prescriptive – you get a weekly shopping list (averaging £50–60 for a family of four and which, brilliantly, you can download online, print and take to the shops), out of which the authors, Rosie Sykes, Polly Russell and Zoe Heron, show you how to make one big meal from scratch, two meals using leftovers, one cheap seasonal supper, one meal largely from your larder, one big meal to freeze and one pudding. It's pretty impressive and a very good idea if you want to cook seasonally/thriftily but don't really know where to start, or don't want to think about it too hard and just want to be told what to do. The book takes you through all fifty-two weeks of the year. I think it's marvellous; I've been cooking from it throughout the writing of this chapter and we're eating really well and, as promised, saving considerable amounts of money.

Seasonal Food

Anyway, eating more cheaply. The best place to start with all of this is by eating seasonally – it's fashionable, it's thrifty, it tastes good because the food's ripe, ready and plentiful, and is less likely to come with giant air miles attached. There is a table below showing what's in season when, but really the best way of finding out is simply to go to your local shops, be they independent or multinationals, and see what's cheapest. Eating seasonally enables you to eat luxuriously: for instance, the asparagus that cost a fortune one month is less than half price the next, and making hollandaise isn't expensive. It's also worth keeping an eye out for gluts of things like tomatoes and courgettes, buying a great big load of them – street markets are the best place to do this – and turning them into sauces, soups, chutneys, pickles and so on. To find locally produced food, go to www.bigbarn.co.uk. Also check out www.bbcgoodfood.com each month for recipes which use food that is currently in season.

Fruit and Veg	Jan	Feb	Mar	Apr	May	Jun	Jul	Aug	Sep	Oct	Nov	Dec
Apples	✓	✓	✓					✓	✓	✓	✓	✓
Asparagus					✓	✓						
Aubergines					✓	✓	✓	✓	✓			
Blackberries								✓	✓	✓		
Broad Beans					✓	✓	✓	✓	✓			
Broccoli	✓	✓	✓					✓	✓	✓	✓	✓
Brussels Sprouts	✓	✓	✓						✓	✓	✓	✓
Cabbage					✓	✓	✓	✓	✓	✓		
Carrots	✓	✓	✓			✓	✓	✓	✓	✓	✓	✓
Cauliflower	✓	✓	✓				✓	✓	✓	✓	✓	✓

Fruit and Veg	Jan	Feb	Mar	Apr	May	Jun	Jul	Aug	Sep	Oct	Nov	Dec
Celery				✓	✓	✓	✓					
Cherries					✓	✓						
Courgettes						✓	✓	✓	✓			
French Beans						✓	✓					
Gooseberries						✓	✓					
Grapes									✓	✓		
Leeks	✓	✓						✓	✓	✓	✓	✓
Lettuce				✓	✓	✓	✓	✓	✓	✓	✓	
Marrows								✓	✓	✓		
New Potatoes					✓	✓	✓	✓	✓			
Onions	✓	✓	✓					✓	✓	✓	✓	✓
Parsnips	✓	✓	✓					✓	✓	✓	✓	✓
Pears	✓	✓	✓						✓	✓	✓	✓
Peas						✓	✓					
Plums									✓	✓		
Potatoes	✓	✓	✓	✓	✓		✓	✓	✓	✓	✓	✓
Pumpkins	✓	✓	✓					✓	✓	✓	✓	✓
Radish			✓	✓	✓	✓	✓	✓	✓	✓	✓	
Raspberries						✓	✓	✓	✓			
Rhubarb				✓	✓	✓	✓	✓	✓			
Runner Beans						✓	✓	✓	✓	✓		
Spinach				✓	✓	✓	✓	✓	✓	✓		
Spring Onions						✓	✓	✓	✓	✓	✓	

Fruit and Veg	Jan	Feb	Mar	Apr	May	Jun	Jul	Aug	Sep	Oct	Nov	Dec
Strawberries						✓	✓	✓	✓	✓		
Swede	✓	✓	✓					✓	✓	✓	✓	✓
Sweetcorn									✓	✓		
Tomatoes				✓	✓	✓	✓	✓	✓	✓		
Turnips	✓	✓							✓	✓	✓	✓
Watercress			✓	✓	✓	✓	✓	✓	✓	✓	✓	

Box Schemes

If you can't be bothered to go round veg shops and supermarkets squinting at the price labels to score the seasonal bargains, think about signing up for an organic box scheme. I am actually in two minds about these. I see that they are wonderful in some respects — eating seasonally, eating organically, helping small suppliers and local farmers, and so on — but I have a problem with them, which is that I don't always eat my box all up and then of course suffer especially acute agonies of guilt when I am chucking out some lovingly hand-reared beetroot, which probably has a pet name, it's been so tenderly cared for.

I also find that what box scheme companies consider to be a 'family'-sized box is often anything but. If there are six of you, say, what are you supposed to do with two little Jerusalem artichokes, or one mango, or a rather undersized lettuce? Perhaps you're culinarily ingenious enough to know how to eke these out into family-sized meals, but I never was. They just used to annoy me, sitting there in the fridge all reproachful and small, and they made me feel wasteful.

Having said that, the best box schemes allow you to customize your order week by week, to share your likes and dislikes with them – so that if, for instance, you're not big on cabbage (a much-maligned vegetable, I feel – Google recipes for Dublin Coddle, a fantastically cheap meal to make and a fabulously delicious one, and see if it changes your mind), they'll substitute it for something you do like. Basically, box schemes are like mobile phone plans: sign up to the wrong one and it ends up being expensive and wasteful, but find your ideal partner and you can't really go very wrong. You need to find a box scheme that is mindful of your preferences and whose website (which you must check every week to avoid unwelcome surprises in your box) publishes the box contents well in advance. There are too many to name here, though I'll mention Abel & Cole (www.abelandcole.co.uk) and Riverford Organics (www.riverford.co.uk), because I've found both to be unusually customer-friendly in the past. A complete list of every single organic box scheme provider in Britain can be found here: www.livingethically.co.uk.

Farmers' Markets

It is also worth familiarizing yourself with your local farmers' market – www.farmersmarkets.net will tell you where your nearest one is. Again, you're buying fresh, seasonal produce direct from the supplier, with no packaging and no air miles, and frankly farmers need all the support they can get. Some people think that farmers' markets are all very well for middle-class rich people playing at being rustic but are not a patch in money-saving terms on the supermarket. This is simply not true: in spring 2007, ten organic apples at Peckham Farmers' Market, for example, came to £1.60, while Sainsbury's sold six (and a vast amount of plastic packaging) for £1.99. The trick, again, is to shop only for what you need. Either go armed with a shopping list or just buy what looks best and most appealing, bearing in mind that things need to go together so that you can build a meal out of them.

Also, farmers' markets sell only what they sell – they don't use all those sly supermarket tricks, like piping in fake bread smells or 3-for-2 offers that lure you into buying stuff you neither want nor need in the mistaken belief that you're getting 'a bargain'. The best trick of all is to turn up just before the market shuts and snap up the stock people are keen to get rid of; they may sell things to you so cheaply, they're practically giving them away. This doesn't work if you want specific items, obviously, but if you're relaxed about what you might have for tonight's supper, you can't go far wrong. Needless to say, shopping ten minutes before closing time is a tried-and-tested trick worth trying anywhere that sells perishable goods, e.g. bakeries.

Growing Your Own

Please skip this bit if you are the green-fingered country type. Not only will I be preaching to the converted, but you might find my idiot-proof guide patronizing or plain simple-minded. It isn't meant to be either – it's just that I was a complete and utter novice, to the point where even books about very basic gardening couldn't help me because I didn't really understand the vocab.

Read on, though, if you're a city person who's never attempted to grow anything more ambitious than a baby spider plant. You're going to be amazed. Growing some of your own food is not only totally cool but incredibly easy and, to my mind, much more quidsworth than box schemes (sainted though they are).

I live in London. I don't have green fingers, to put it mildly – in fact, I appear to have fingers of doom when it comes to growing things. I have a useless, tiny patch of paved garden, which is north-facing and apparently functions as some sort of snail commune/Shangri-La. But I do, at the front of my house, have railings which I can hang tubs off, windowsills and space for some terracotta pots by the front door. I live in a household of six permanently hungry people and 'entertain' once or twice a week. I have been growing my own salad, in said tubs (two of them), and have not yet had to supplement it with those chlorine-washed, nutrition-free, plastic-bagged leaves from the supermarket. I am inordinately proud of my salad-growing achievements – and my salad is seriously delicious, as well as completely organic.

This is what I did to induce salad bliss: I ordered seedlings from Sarah Raven's Kitchen & Garden (www.sarahraven.com), specifically a selection called Foodies' Salad Collection. I got ten seedlings for £9.50: two each of mizuna, oak leaf lettuce, mustard 'Golden Streaks' and lettuce 'Cocarde', plus a nasturtium 'Black Velvet' (very beautiful) and mustard 'Osaka Purple'. They dispatched the seedlings by post in mid-April, brilliantly packed in little bump-proof pods. The collections might change each year but the principle remains the same:

You unpack them and sit the pods in the sink for a bit, so they can have a drink.

You get tubs, pots or whatever.

You put broken bits of terracotta over the drainage holes, then top up with compost.

You plant the seedlings. They look really pathetic and small and too widely spaced out, but you have faith.

You water them devotedly every day – and, incredibly to simple me, within a couple of weeks you have different varieties of DELICIOUS salad that just keep on coming throughout the summer.

That's it. It is insanely easy. What you then do is either a) 'cut and come again', i.e. chop off the whole lettuce and eat it, and wait ten days or so for another one to be ready (which is fine, because you have several other lettuces to be getting on with), or b) pick off about half the leaves, so if you have twelve leaves you pick six, and so on. This makes the plant stronger, but isn't half as satisfying as seeing the whole thing boinging up again within days. So there you go: more salad than you know what to do with, for months on end, for £9.50. Added advantage: children are really keen on eating stuff they've grown, or helped grow, or at least monitored.

I shan't bang on endlessly about this, but I must just also crow about my herbs, also from Sarah Raven and also £9.50 – flat-leaf parsley, wild rocket, chervil (so delicious in omelettes), basil and chives. Exactly the same principle and not only wonderful-tasting but the most fabulous

bargain when you consider how much one sweaty little ungenerously sized plastic bag of herbs costs in supermarkets. I also grow thyme, rosemary and Moroccan mint (for tea and the best fresh mint sauce). If you grow these herbs from seed, which I wasn't confident enough to do this time around, you'll be talking about spending pence for a veritable bounty of goodness, but I still think £19 isn't bad for a whole summer of green leafy salad 'n' herb abundance.

I must also eagerly direct you to www. rocketgardens.co.uk, which won a Good Housekeeping Food Award in 2007. They bill themselves as the UK's 'only supplier of instant kitchen gardens' and are absolutely wonderful if, like me, you don't think of yourself as quite competent enough to grow everything from scratch: i.e. from seed. They tailor their instant gardens to the amount of space you have available, whether it's a

patch of actual garden or just a little window box. I ordered the Instant Patio Container Garden* (£36.99: the price of two weeks' worth of organic veg boxes), which comprised enough tomatoes, green courgettes, yellow courgettes, green beans, runner beans, mixed lettuces, mizuna, rainbow chard, rocket and garden peas to keep a large family of famished Vikings going all summer. To give you an idea, there are twenty little rocket plants, so we're talking quite a lot of containers. The company also does a windowsill garden (which produces a surprisingly bountiful amount) and some charming children's gardens, as well as bigger ones.

I'm not going to give out endless lists of specific website addresses, either here or throughout this book, because everyone knows how to Google, and besides, both the companies I've mentioned have comprehensive instructions about growing their fruits, herbs and vegetables on their own sites, but if you want to learn more about this, you might like to have a look at www.windowbox.com, or ease yourself in gently by growing mustard and cress. I know it sounds slightly silly, but if you've never grown anything before and feel nervous, this is an excellent place to start, much as walking (and see pages 174–5) is brilliant exercise if you're scared of the gym. Brilliant mode of transport too, of course – more on this later.

* *Available in June 08. Check the website for the latest products.*

How to Grow Mustard and Cress

You will need: an old yogurt pot; kitchen roll; cotton wool; a packet of mustard and cress seeds

Wash the yogurt pot and remove any outside wrapper. Wet some scrunched-up kitchen roll and put this into the pot, then add a thin, damp layer of cotton wool on top, leaving a gap of about 2cm below the rim of the pot. Sprinkle the seeds on the cotton wool and press them down lightly. Leave the pot in a warm, light place and after seven days your mustard and cress should start to sprout. Make sure the cotton wool remains damp and add a little water if necessary.

Allotments

This section wouldn't be complete without making mention of allotments – like gold dust in urban areas, but still worth investigating, and not necessarily as hard to come by as you may have heard. Contact your local council, as they theoretically have a statutory obligation to provide a sufficient number of plots. If there's a waiting list, get yourself on it; it may not take too long if you're open to plot-sharing or renovating a disused allotment. Search for allotments around the UK on www.allotments-uk.com and read all about the joys of this kind of self-sufficiency at the invaluable www.allotment.org.uk (a personal site, despite its suffix). I know people who practically live for their allotments and for the unbeatable combination of fresh air, free food, exercise and the sense of achievement they provide.

Free Food

I should also mention free food, as in food that grows freely and you can pick, but beyond blackberries for crumble, delicious nettles for soup (www.nettles.org.uk) and wild garlic (it lives near bluebells and the smell leads you to it), I've never foraged for my dinner. The National Trust has published a brilliant book on the subject called *Wild Food*, £6.99, which shows you how to find and cook anything from nuts and seeds to flowers and mushrooms. You might also try and pick up a copy of the hippie classic *Food for Free* by Richard Mabey (Collins, various editions at various prices). Needless to say, please arm yourself with a good guide if you go mushroom-picking: free 'shrooms are great, death by poisoning less so.

But anyway, back to our imaginary supper. What to eat? You've procured, grown or picked your vegetables, but you're perhaps not vegetarian – not that you have to be to concoct a lovely dinner without meat.

I must just detour slightly here and offer up a little song of praise to Indian vegetarian cookery. I have a dim memory of the trouble Edwina Currie, then health minister, once got into, not only about eggs and salmonella but about how poor people had terrible diets. 'Middle-class harpy!' the commentators cried. 'They eat what they can afford to eat! Leave them alone!' But I remember thinking – grim as I found Ms Currie (grimmer still when it turned out she was knobbing John Major, or rather that he was knobbing her) – that she was absolutely right and there was no need for poor Britons to eat a million times worse than poor Indians, or to make themselves pasty and obese and to turn their children into blimps, and to spend a ton of money in the process.

It is a complete fallacy – though a very enduring one – that 'healthy' food is more expensive. This is simply not true – it's not even close to being true. Healthy food tastes different because it's not loaded with chemicals and additives, and if you're used to eating heavily processed, additive-rich rubbish, you may not like the way it tastes, in the same way that people used to guzzling Diet Coke (not cheap) always have temper tantrums and wail absurdly about 'not liking the taste' when you suggest they drink water (free). That's an entirely separate issue. Money-wise, though, there's no contest. You could feed six people rice, dhal and raita for less than the price of one lamentable frozen pizza or one crappy little ready meal, and if you had the time you could make chapattis alongside (ingredients: flour and water), which would cost you about another 25p. You'd have not only something delicious and nutritious that everyone liked, but plenty of change from a fiver – a bag of red lentils currently costs around 80p to 90p at the supermarket and just over half that at my local Indian grocer's (tip: always buy pulses, spices, rice, chutneys and condiments at an Indian grocer's – they're literally half price, and fresher because of the high turnover. This is also true of enormous bunches of coriander, of ginger, garlic and fresh chillies, and of those amazing Alfonso mangoes in season – a revelation after the hard, indigestible, overpriced little supermarket bullets*).

I appreciate that we live in Britain, not India, but we do keep being told that curry is now our national dish, and I think it's about time we wised up to the fact that Indian food is quick, easy to make if you stick to the basics and unbelievably cheap. I had a brilliant dinner party a few months ago – I couldn't be bothered to go to the supermarket and I was trying to spend minimal amounts of cash, so I went to my local Indian shop in Drummond Street, in London, and fed twelve people a most delicious, fragrant, luxurious Indian vegetarian feast for £20 (and I had change) – not including wine, but including a splendiferous mango curry that certain people still bang on about (they were in season, about to be overripe, and you could buy whole

* *Turkish supermarkets are also brilliant for very cheap, very fresh herbs and vegetables.*

boxes for very little). So this is my top tip, if you're trying to eat lavishly on a tight budget, and it's a very good one, though I say so myself.

Can't cook Indian food, you say. Well, this isn't really a cookery book, but here are the two I use all the time: 1) *30-minute Indian* by Sunil Vijayakar (a cook of genius), published by Hamlyn, £5.99 and 2) *Cooking Like Mummyji* by Vicky Bhogal (a masterpiece on the subject of the kind of food my granny used to make, all of it easy to prepare and accessibly written up), published by Simon & Schuster, £14.99.

A Delicious Vegetable Curry, with variations

This is a very basic, very aromatic curry sauce, to which you can add any number of vegetables. It'll taste fine if you chuck in whatever you have lying around in your fridge and sublime if you lovingly seek out spankingly fresh veg.

Serves 4–6

1 medium onion, chopped

3 tablespoons vegetable oil (I use groundnut)

a thumb-sized piece of ginger, peeled and coarsely grated

2 green chillies, deseeded and finely chopped

½ teaspoon ground cumin

½ teaspoon ground coriander

2 cloves

1 stick of cinnamon

seeds from 6–8 cardamom pods

a pinch of turmeric

salt

2 large tins chopped tomatoes

1. Fry the onion in the oil on a medium heat until soft.

2. Add the ginger, chillies, spices and a good pinch of salt, turn the heat down a bit and leave to cook for 5 minutes, so the spices give up their flavours. Stir things around to make sure the mixture doesn't burn. If it looks like it's sticking, add a few drops of water.

3. Add the chopped tomatoes.

4. At some point within the next 5–10 minutes the oil and the tomatoey bit will sort of separate. This means your sauce is ready.

5. To this basic sauce, you can add any vegetable, or combination of vegetables, you like, bearing in mind that hard veg (e.g. potatoes) will need longer to cook than soft veg (e.g. spinach) and will therefore need to go in first. So, add your chosen veg to the basic sauce and another good pinch of salt, stir it all about, then pour in a mug or so of water if things look too dry or you want a runnier curry.

6. Simmer until the vegetables are cooked, which, depending on what you've chosen, will be anything from 5 to 15 minutes. You might consider any of the following, either singly or in combinations:

* potatoes, cut into cubes
* leaf spinach
* frozen peas
* home-made cheese (paneer; see pages 50–52)
* green beans, cut into lengths
* whole baby shallots, peeled
* carrots, cut into slices
* cauliflower florets
* mushrooms
* cabbage, shredded
* courgettes, cut into slices
* pumpkin, cut into cubes
* squash, cut into cubes

Also:

  * Add a mug of washed red lentils to the base, top up with water and you have dhal. Top up with more water and you have lentil soup.

  * Use only 2 tablespoons of tomatoes and add a can of coconut milk, in which case keep the heat low and forget about the oil

separating. You have a yummy, more southern Indian base, which will taste completely different.

* Experiment with adding a pinch or two of garam masala or tandoori masala 10 minutes or so before the end of cooking for yet another couple of flavour variations.

* Add leftover cooked meat – chicken and lamb work especially well – to the vegetable mixture and warm through. Even a very small bit of meat will make a difference.

* The coconut base is especially delicious with added prawns; it's also fantastic with leftover roast lamb and spinach.

* You can add fresh fish, but make sure it's something sturdy that holds its shape.

* You can add a couple of generous tablespoons of yogurt to the basic mix for a tangier taste, but keep the heat right down to stop it curdling.

* Don't think that just adding a load of chopped potato is going to be boring and bland – it's delicious.

* Frozen peas + home-made cheese (see pages 50–52) = mattar paneer; spinach + home-made cheese = sag paneer.

* You can beef up and eke out any of the tomato-based curries (but not the coconut ones) by chucking in a can of rinsed chickpeas; add water if it's too thick.

* If the cupboard is really bare, you can do just chickpeas and a minute amount of green veg – very hearty and comforting.

* Egg curry (my favourite): make the curry using the tomato base and add chopped potato. About 10 minutes before you want to eat, add halved hard-boiled eggs. Spoon the sauce over so they're immersed and heat through gently. Benefits hugely from chopped coriander leaves scattered over the top.

Meat

Right, rant over and back to the world of omnivores. Happily for the thrifty-minded, cheap cuts of meat are tremendously fashionable.

Beef

Let's start here, where the cheapest cuts make the best comfort food. This is stuff you throw together in the morning and leave to simmer all day, so that you come home to a feast. If you're worried about leaving the gas on, look at second-hand slow-cookers on eBay — you can usually pick one up for between £5 and £10.

❚❚ **The chuck** section comes from the neck and shoulders of the beast. It is cheap and delicious, but needs slow cooking, as do most of the cheaper cuts. Use it for casseroles, stews, some curries, braising.

❚❚ **Shin and leg** cuts are great for stews and for making stock.

❚❚ **Breast and flank** cuts include flank steak, skirt steak, hanger steak, brisket and short ribs, and again are good for casseroles, stews, mincing, braising, slow-roasting and pot-roasting.

❚❚ **Flank and skirt** steak make good steak-steak (i.e. pan-fried), but they need your help and that means a marinade to transform them from tough to tender and from potentially horsy to completely heavenly. There are hundreds of recipes online.

There is excellent advice on how to transform these otherwise tough, fibrous cuts of meat into meltingly tender, delicious dinners at www.seekingsources.com/braising_foods.htm. For an extremely useful article and good starting point, see also www.getrichslowly. org/blog/2007/01/19/making-the-most-of-cheap-cuts-of-beef.

Lamb

I love the fact that all lamb is free-range. Cheap bits:

❙❙ **Scrag** (the upper part of the neck) is great for stews and casseroles.

❙❙ **Neck** is a tougher cut that is generally used for stewing and mincing and is the traditional base for Lancashire Hotpot.

❙❙ **Shoulder** is absolutely delicious slow-roasted, but can also be diced and used in our old friends the stew and the curry.

❙❙ **Breast** is versatile and can be used for mince, kebabs and burgers.

❙❙ **And don't forget mutton**, which is cheap, fantastically flavourful and enjoying something of a second coming among foodies. See www.muttonrenaissance.org.uk – launched by the Prince of Wales, if you please – for detailed information on this much underrated meat.

Pork

❙❙ **Pork belly** is the most delicious meat and rewards slow-cooking with sensational taste and texture (as any Chinese person knows). You can cook it for ages and it never dries out, but retains a succulence (to use one of my least favourite words) that I personally am mad about.

❙❙ **Pork shoulder** makes fantastic slow-roasts.

❙❙ **The collar** and neck parts make spare ribs, chops, boneless steaks, mince and diced pork.

❙❙ **Cheek meat** is possibly the most delicious cut of all – dirt cheap and on the menu at some of London's best restaurants.

❙❙ **And streaky bacon** – the cheapest cut – is to my mind the best, thrift or no thrift.

A Delicious Stew, with variations

Serves 4–5

2 onions, roughly chopped
1 tablespoon each olive oil and butter
1 sprig of thyme or 2 bay leaves
800g stewing steak in chunks (chuck, shin, flank or skirt)
1 heaped tablespoon seasoned flour
2 parsnips, thickly sliced
4 carrots, thickly sliced
2 tablespoons tomato purée
1 garlic clove, chopped
1 can of Guinness or Pale Ale or ½ bottle cheap red wine
285ml water or stock
salt and freshly ground black pepper
a handful of parsley and dill mixed, chopped

1. Fry the onions in the oil and butter mixture in a large cast-iron stew pot.

2. Add the thyme or bay leaves.

3. Toss the meat in the seasoned flour and add along with the parsnips, carrots, tomato purée, garlic, alcohol and stock.

4. Season with salt and pepper, stir it up and bring to the boil.

5. Either simmer at the merest blipping burp on the hob or, when boiling, transfer to an oven preheated to 160°C/300°F/gas mark 2.

6. Cook for 3–4 hours depending on the toughness of the meat. It is done when the meat starts falling apart when you try to break up the chunks.

7. Stew is always much better if you cook it the day before you want to eat it. The next day you can skim off any excess fat, then bring it to a simmer again, sprinkle with the parsley and dill and serve with mashed potato.

Variations:

* You could mix in cooked haricot beans.

* All stews are great with root vegetables, so besides the carrots and parsnips you could add or substitute: turnips, celeriac, fennel, beetroot, Jerusalem artichokes.

* You can make it more Italian-tasting by following the wine option and adding a large can of tomatoes and a small can of anchovies. Garnish with black olives and finely chopped parsley or torn-up basil leaves.

* Lamb will work just as well, but don't use beer. Instead, try cooking lamb scrag, neck or shoulder or mutton as above with wine. For a vaguely French Provençal stew, try adding some brown lentils halfway through the cooking. For a Middle Eastern stew, fry the onion first with a mixture of 1 teaspoon each of ground cumin, cinnamon and allspice and use water instead of wine, omitting the parsnips and adding 2 aubergines in chunks halfway through cooking.

* Pork works best with Chinese flavours, so don't use wine or beer, but add a swig of sherry alongside the water or stock, plus some star anise if you have it and 150ml soy sauce. Add a chopped finger of root ginger with the garlic. Garnish at the end with finely chopped coriander.

Offal

I've become slightly queasy about offal in recent years, which is a shame –
as a child, one of my absolutely favourite things was brains in black butter*
and brains masala (which my mother made, and which is an amazing sort
of thought since she is these days fastidiously vegetarian). I've made myself
feel quite hungry thinking about it, actually. I think offal has suffered
tremendously from the fact that we now all anthropomorphize animals
as a matter of course – oh, the little calfy's brain, waah, the little lamby's
kidneys. It's really rather pathetic. Either you eat animals or you don't, and
if you do, there isn't a huge amount to be gained, frankly, by coming over
all squeamish about some parts while happily chomping down on others
– it is surely unnecessarily winsome (though I am winsome too – I can't
do tongue). Plus, if you eat sausages, you've eaten penis, anus and eyeball,
so, you know . . . Anyway, offal is incredibly nutritious, incredibly cheap
and eating it up means that none of the animal goes to waste. Also, it can
taste sublime – just think of oxtail. See the American www.offalgood.com
for a guide to good guts and also the BBC's beginner's guide to offal at www.
bbc.co.uk/food/recipes/mostof_offal.shtml, which contains some great
recipes. If you want more, it's worth tracking down Fergus Henderson's
seminal *Nose to Tail Eating* (Bloomsbury, £16.99) for wonderful recipes.

These cookery books I keep mentioning are only recommendations, and
are available from your local library, but there are literally millions of free
recipes available online. If you're overwhelmed by choice, www.epicurious.
com is a good place to start – it is a repository of tens of thousands of
fantastic recipes, written by greedy people for greedy people. There

---

* *I can't tell you how delicious these were/are. Simon Hopkinson has a recipe for them
in his* Roast Chicken and Other Stories *(Ebury, £12), which also has chapters on
liver, kidneys, tripe and sweetbreads. I'm not suggesting you buy all these books,
by the way – not when libraries have photocopiers, or you have pen and paper.*

are also hundreds of absolutely fantastic food and cookery websites and blogs – too many to list, but here are a handful of my personal favourites:

http://chocolateandzucchini.com
Written (in English) by a young Frenchwoman who lovingly chronicles everything she eats, cooks, buys and bakes. Wonderful recipes and written with real verve, like the best kind of cookery book.

www.chow.com
Huge site with recipes, blogs, message boards and videos – an extremely useful resource.

www.101cookbooks.com
An online recipe journal, mainly vegetarian. The recipes are great and there are also forums.

http://theendivechronicles.com
I just really like the recipes on here.

www.pinchmysalt.com
Another cookery diary with lovely recipes – homely and chic at the same time.

www.cookingforengineers.com
One for those of you with an analytical mind. Explains the hows brilliantly, but also throws in the whys.

www.foodwishes.blogspot.com
Video recipes!

http://startcooking.com
One for kitchen novices.

Having said all of that, my main tip about meat is: eat less of it. And be intelligent about how you use it. If you don't buy meat for a couple of weeks and suddenly have a violently carnivorous urge, for instance, don't just buy a fillet steak, cook it and eat it – feeds one. Do something ingenious with it: slice it thinly, for example, and turn it into a hot Thai beef salad – feeds four (see the box below for a delicious recipe). If you like eating meat often, go for the cheap cuts. If you like eating meat as a treat, buy the best you can afford but eke it out.

Hot Thai Beef Salad

Serves 4

3 tablespoons tamari soy sauce
3 tablespoons groundnut oil
2 tablespoons fish sauce (nam pla)
juice of 2 limes
100g steak (sirloin, fillet), sliced across the grain as thinly as possible
a 2.5cm piece of fresh ginger, peeled and grated
1 teaspoon sugar
2 garlic cloves, smashed
2–3 fresh red chillies, finely sliced
50ml stock, made with Marigold bouillon powder
oil for frying
25g creamed coconut, grated
flat-leaf parsley, torn into pieces
cos lettuce leaves, torn into pieces
2 spring onions, sliced
handful of fresh coriander, chopped

1. Whisk together 1 tablespoon each of tamari, groundnut oil, fish sauce and lime juice. Pour the mixture over the sliced steak, squish it around in the liquid and leave to marinate for an hour or so.

2. To make the dressing, put the remaining tamari, oil and fish sauce into a bowl and whisk in 2 tablespoons of lime juice, the ginger, sugar, garlic, chillies and stock.

3. Pour a dash of oil into a frying pan over a medium heat. When the oil is hot, add the sliced beef and stir-fry briskly until the outside of the meat is browned.

4. Pour over the dressing and when it boils (it takes seconds), stir in the creamed coconut and parsley.

5. Serve the beef on top of the lettuce leaves, sprinkled with sliced spring onions and coriander.

Fish

On to fish. Fish is rather tricky. Farming fish is bad. Catching wild fish is bad. Fish are running out; their ecosystems are messed up. Water is polluted. Greenpeace advises us to eat less fish, but we all seem to be eating more: so yummy, so good for you, and available free to anyone with a fishing rod. Wild fish are obviously a finite resource and it's difficult to catch them in a sustainable way. Farming fish, which detractors liken to mining, is the only way to meet demand, especially when it comes to top-of-the-food-chain carnivorous fish, such as tuna and salmon. The problem is that farming fish has its environmental impact – polluting waters, depleting wild fish stocks (used for feeds), transmitting disease and parasites to wild species, and endangering other sea animals to prevent them feeding on captive fish. It's a bit of a bummer, really, the whole fish situation.

I don't want to preach, so if you're unconcerned enough by all of this not to alter your fish-eating habits, then carry on as you were. Otherwise, what with 70 per cent of the world's fish stocks now described by the Food and Agriculture Organization as fully fished, overfished or depleted, it seems glaringly obvious that we should all be making an effort to eat sustainable fish. According to Greenpeace, this means a) it's come from a sustainable fishery* and b) it's caught using fishing methods that don't damage or destroy the marine environment or harm other sea creatures.

This is very nice, but it's actually really difficult to identify fish that come from sustainable sources. This is a vast and complex subject, and if you want to read more about it you might like to stop off at www.fishonline.org, which goes into all of this in great detail, gives advice and publishes lists of fish we should eat and fish we should avoid.

---

* This means it adheres to practices that can be maintained indefinitely without reducing the fish in question's ability to maintain its population.

Meanwhile, here are some further guidelines:

- **Eat less of the big fish** like salmon, tuna, swordfish and sharks. These are the most vulnerable populations and also the ones that live the longest, have the most fat and accumulate the most toxins over their lifespan.

- **Eat smaller fish** like clams, oysters, molluscs, anchovies and sardines. Smaller species are more abundant and reproduce faster, so are less endangered. They also have less fat and don't accumulate as many toxins. And, happily for us, they are cheaper.

- **In the UK, very few fish are farmed sustainably**. The best options are line-caught mackerel and sea bass, farmed mussels, rod- and line-caught tuna and herring. Purse-seined herring from Cornwall is also a good choice (and helps the Cornish fishing industry, which needs it).

- **Marks & Spencer** have invested considerable time and effort in improving the way the fish they sell is caught and farmed. Not all fish sold by M&S are from fully sustainable sources, but, according to Greenpeace, they are certainly the best available from a UK supermarket.

- **Your local fishmonger** may sell fish from sustainable sources – ask.

- **Always ask** the person you buy fish from where and how their fish is caught. If they can't tell you or if you are not completely satisfied with their answer, don't buy the fish.

- **Here is the link to an online article** about a couple who own the UK's first organic carp farm and claim it is one of the most sustainable sources of fish out there www.bbc.co.uk/theoneshow/article/2008/04/ls_carp.shtml. Apparently carp tastes a bit like sea bass, and film director Mike Leigh is a big fan.

- **A useful website** is www.fishonline.org/search/simple. Just enter a type of fish and you can find out how it is caught and how sustainable it is.

Dairy

There's a whole slew of other stuff you can make, including your own ingredients. It is, for instance, surprisingly easy to make your own cheese. You need milk, obviously – any kind, really: cow (the stuff that comes in bottles is fine if you don't have your own dairy herd), goat, sheep, buffalo, or even dried milk. If you are making soft or curd cheese, you can use natural live yogurt or lemon juice (see below) as a culture. For anything more complicated, you will need a starter culture – this is basically helpful bacteria – which you can obtain online with ease, from suppliers such as www.cheesemaking.co.uk (who stock everything you might conceivably need, not just cultures) and www.cheeseyogurtessentials.com. You may also need rennet, depending on what type of cheese you're making, and might want salt, herbs or other flavourings. There is masses about this online, not least at www. cheesemaking.com (Ricki, its creator, is the US Queen of Home-Made Cheese), but also at our aforementioned friend www.allotment.org.uk.

Here is the recipe that started me off – I'm afraid I can't remember where it's from, because I cut and pasted it into my online cookery book (and I urge you to make a cookery book out of all the recipes brilliant amateur cooks volunteer online – not only is it free, but it turns into the Bible. I use a Mac and the software that comes with it makes creating a webpage or blog almost embarrassingly easy – the advantage then is that you can share your page/blog with family and friends. There are an almost infinite number of recipes, food blogs and brilliant food writing available on line, cost 0 pence. See pages 170–72 for a selection of my favourite free online reading, on everything from cookery to design to fashion to politics).

How to Make Really, Really Easy Cheese

So we're making white cheese, the simplest kind of all. Think ricotta, curd cheese or paneer – same kind of texture and same kind of clean, very mild taste.

For 400g

You will need: a large pan; a wooden spoon; a colander; a largish piece of muslin – nick one from a baby and double it up if it seems especially thin or worn; a bowl to sit the colander in; string; 2 litres organic whole milk; 4–5 tablespoons freshly squeezed lemon juice

1. Pour the milk into a large pan that allows room for boiling. Bring it to a rolling boil over medium heat. Stir frequently with a wooden spoon to prevent sticking. Squeeze the lemon juice while it's warming up.

2. When the milk boils, remove it from the heat. Immediately but slowly add the lemon juice – don't chuck it in in one fell swoop.

3. While you add the lemon juice, gently move the wooden spoon through the hot milk in one direction, in a sort of scraping motion.

After a few seconds, you should see the milk splitting into lumps of curd and watery whey. These curds are your home-made cheese.

4. Cover the pan and set aside for 2 hours. This allows the curds to settle properly (note: I've left it for a mere hour and it's been fine). When the curds have settled, line the colander with muslin.

5. Place the colander in the sink, or in a large bowl if you intend to collect the whey. Slowly pour the curdled milk into the colander. When all the liquid is drained off, gather the corners of the muslin together to form a snug bag. Tie the bag containing the curds with string.

6. Hang the bag over the sink or a bowl to let any remaining liquid whey drip off. Leave hanging for 3 hours, then your home-made cheese is ready for eating. It keeps well in the fridge for 3–4 days.

See? It's incredibly easy. I don't want to sound obsessed by curry or anything, but if you grew some spinach, you could rustle up some sag paneer for literally a few pence.

How to Make Even Easier Cheese

I also like making labneh, the creamy Middle Eastern cheese that is unbelievably delicious eaten with flat bread and meze, or spread on bruschetta (which you make by buying stale bread for cheap; my local deli sometimes just gives it away when they're about to close) and topped with olive oil and herbs. This is really so utterly simple that a child could do it, and in my house they frequently do. There are just two ingredients: six cups of good-quality full-fat yogurt (I use sheep's, and some jaunty coloured measuring cups from Lakeland, www.lakeland.co.uk), and 2 teaspoons of salt. You need some muslin again, plus a whisk and a bowl.

Simply put the yogurt into the bowl and whisk in the salt for a minute or so, then line the colander with the muslin, gather up the corners, as in the above recipe, tie up the bundle with string, hang it over a bowl to catch the drips and leave it to do its thing overnight (for about 12 hours). That is it. It's very good.

How to Make Butter

It follows that making your own butter is very simple too, though it isn't especially economical unless you can get free cream from somewhere, or at least discounted cream – if it's about to go past its sell-by date and is being sold off cheaply, turn it into butter and freeze it. Here's what you do (and this is another good thing to make with children):

You need a big jar with a lid, a bowl and either serious elbow grease or an electric whisk or food processor (put on the plastic blades for the latter), as well as however much double cream you have to hand – say 285ml.

Let the cream come to room temperature – it won't work if you don't. You want it to be about 20°Celsius.

Now either half-fill the jar with the cream and shake like mad for about 40 minutes or, rather more speedily, whisk the cream, either in the bowl with the electric whisk or in the food processor using the plastic blades. It'll turn (obviously) into whipped cream and then start getting thicker and stiffer. Watch it carefully at this point – I switch my food processor to 'pulse' here.

The cream will start going yellow and grainy. The grains are the start of the butter; the liquid is the buttermilk. Slow down your whisking – the butter will suddenly clump.

Drain off as much of the buttermilk as you can (use it in cooking – it's brilliant for making soda bread).

 Wash your butter (yes, really). Put it into a bowl and add very cold water – if it's not cold, it will melt the butter. Press the butter together with a wooden spoon so it makes one big lump. Press out any remaining buttermilk.

 Drain off the water carefully and repeat until the water runs clear. This could take up to 15 goes – just keep at it.

 Now use your hands, or the back of a pair of spoons, to squeeze and shape the butter to ensure that all the water is out.

 Add salt, herbs or whatever else you fancy, and shape it into a lovely little log. Voila – home-made butter. It'll keep for 3 months in the freezer (note: it keeps better if it's unsalted).

How to Make Yogurt

It is also easy to make yogurt at home, either using live yogurt to kick the process off or buying a culture online or at the health food shop (you only do this once). All the information you need is widely available, including from http://healthycooking. suite101.com/article.cfm/making_yogurt_at_home. If you want to see how it's made with your very own eyes, visit the brilliant www.videojug.com, which  is a website containing thousands of videos on every conceivable subject, from how to snorkel to how to get the perfect smoky eye (and see page 193 for more on terrific, free online make-up demonstrations) to, yes, how to make yogurt: www.videojug.com/film/how-to-make-greek-yoghurt.

Jams, Chutneys and Preserves

Unusually, I haven't come across any especially inspiring websites on this most marvellous topic, although VideoJug, which I mentioned above, is keen to show you how to make strawberry jam. But websites aren't always necessary – not when the magnificent Marguerite Patten is about, or rather her brilliant *Jams, Preserves and Chutneys* is (part of the Basic Basics series, published by Grub Street, £7.99). I love all of this stuff: the thrift of it, but also the beautiful, Victorian-seeming (as she points out) abundance of having shelves lined with stores of preserves, and the joy of turning cheap gluts of fruit and vegetables into wonderful and delicious treats. I cannot recommend this book enough: it turned me – I don't like sticky things and I'm scared of getting burned after an unfortunate incident with a chip pan years ago – into an adequate jam-maker in one afternoon. It transpires that making jam is really not difficult at all – who knew? My newly found skills were compounded by my friend Juliet's genius marmalade recipe, which follows. It will stop you dead in your tracks: goodbye, bought marmalade (even Cooper's Oxford); hello, home-made perfection. And – easy, even for a little marmalade virgin such as I (as Lorelei Lee might have put it).

Marmalade

This is a fresh-tasting, sharp marmalade, not too dark or bitter.

Makes 8 small/6 medium jars
2kg Seville oranges
3 lemons
4kg preserving sugar

1. Put all the fruit into a preserving pan or large saucepan and cover with water, then put a plate inside the pan to stop them bobbing up. Bring to the boil and simmer for 1½ hours. Take them out of the water and cool. You can do this the day before if you like.

2. Measure out the orangey water so that you have around 3 litres (this is not that important, as if you have too much water you can just evaporate it later).

3. Cut the oranges and lemons in half. Scoop out the pips and pulp, placing them in the orangey water, and boil for about 15 minutes. While you are doing that, cut the peel into shreds the size and shape you like.

4. Sieve the boiled orange water, pips and pulp into a bowl. Pour the liquid back into the preserving pan. Add the sugar and peel, and bring to a boil. Boil for 15 minutes, after which you can start testing for a set.

5. Testing for a set is not as complicated as it sounds. If you have a suitable thermometer, put it in the middle of the pan. You should have a set when it reads 105°C (220°F). If you don't have a thermometer, put a saucer into the freezer to cool down. When you think the marmalade is ready, take the saucer out and put about ½ teaspoon of marmalade on to the plate. Allow it to cool. Push your finger through the marmalade: if it wrinkles, you've got a set. If not, boil for a further 5 minutes and test again. Sometimes it takes 17 minutes to set, sometimes 25.

6. While the marmalade is still hot, bottle in sterilized jars (run them through the dishwasher when it's full anyway).

Packed Lunch

People spend an insane-seeming amount of money on lunch every day – I don't mean lunch in restaurants, I mean lunch at the sandwich shop or takeout place. I haven't worked in an office for a while, so I am always astonished at the prices: it seems impossible to get a halfway decent sandwich for much under £3 at any of the big chains. Chuck in a brownie or a fruit salad, a bottle of mineral water and maybe a coffee, and you're talking about £7. That's £35 a week, and you can add another £10 on top if you have a Starbucks habit – to say nothing of a crisp or muffin or soft drink habit, which'll cost you extra. It makes no sense: it's not like everyone's so rich they can afford it, or like they wouldn't rather spend the money on other stuff, or like the food in question is so dazzlingly good that no one minds paying these ridiculous amounts for it.

Time, I think, for a return to the home-made sandwich – your perfect sandwich, created by you, with no question mark over dodgy ingredients – brought to work in a brown paper bag. Or a salad, or noodles, or whatever you fancy. It takes ten minutes of work in the morning and will save you a fortune, plus it'll free up the time you spend queuing in the sandwich shop, feeling bad-tempered and hurried. If you spend £7 a day on lunch — assuming that's what it evens out at: i.e. you may spend less but sometimes go and sit down and have a pizza with colleagues — and an extra £10 a week on coffee and/or muffins and/or chocolate bars and/or crisps (easily done, when the smallest, most basic latte costs upwards of £1.50), you're spending £2,340 a year just on eating at work. One word: don't. And, for heaven's sake, drink tap water. It's good for you, it can seriously help control your weight, it's thirst-quenching like nothing else on earth is and it's free.

Eating Out

My second plea concerns eating out. We all know where our local cheap restaurants are, but I don't know that everyone is quite aware of the incredible bargains you can get if you go for the set lunch at some of the country's most exclusive and garlanded restaurants. Please check them out. Dinner for two at such places in London could easily set you back £120 a head; the set lunch is usually between the £20 and £40 mark, and we're talking serious food, with no corners cut. If you're going somewhere special for a meal and want to have the full extravagant, luxey experience without feeling like you might have to remortgage your house, go for lunch, and remember to book well in advance, especially if there's a party of you (going for lunch at posh restaurants is the best way of going out for a family celebration — it feels really special and treat-like, but nobody cries at the bill).

The following websites specialize in restaurant discounts: www.lastminute.com, www.toptable.com and www.5pm.co.uk.

Picnics

My next eating-out tip is picnics. Everyone likes the idea, but not so much the reality, whereas in fact picnics can be absolutely wonderful with a bit of forward planning. I'm not going to tell you how to have a picnic, but I will just mention extending the picnic idea past the lunchtime-in-the-park version. Night-time picnics, either in the park or in a field or on a beach or in a back garden, are wildly romantic and much cheaper to organize than an equivalent dinner party (also, people have lower expectations: anything that isn't a curly ham sandwich is greeted with rapture). Candlelit picnics for two make brilliant first (or third, or two hundredth) dates. Don't be limited by the seasons either – my favourite recent picnic was on Bonfire Night, on top of Primrose Hill, in the freezing darkness and with fireworks going off all around us. The children were bundled up like Eskimos, we had a tarpaulin as well as a blanket to lay on the ground and home-made hot dogs (kept warm in layers of foil) and chocolate cake, with spiced hot apple juice (in flasks) and mulled wine (ditto) to drink. It was one of the loveliest nights ever, and since we made the food, it cost about £10.

Chickens

Oh, and another thing: chickens. As in keeping them. This is not actually especially economical (people used to keep them for thrift reasons when eggs were rationed, which is obviously no longer the case). It is cheaper and less of a hassle to go and buy eggs from the shop – even free-range or organic eggs. However, I still think keeping chickens is pretty cool, as is making omelettes from your own eggs. I've toyed with the idea myself, but I'm not mad about birds (I hate their feet, also their beaks, also their eyes), so I've – ho ho – chickened out. But if you have no such issues, and if you like chickens – and, obviously, the glorious eggs they'll provide you with in perpetuity – and if you don't mind an initially fairly hefty outlay in exchange for peace of mind (you get big, fat, healthy, vaccinated chickens, organic feed, a brilliantly designed chicken house called an Eglu, a fox-proof chicken run, a feeder and drinker and a book explaining what to do), then have a look at www.omlet.co.uk. At the time of writing, all of this chicken goodness would set you back between £300 and £400. Obviously, this is really targeted at urbanites – if you live in the country and can score some chickens locally and knock up a hen house yourself, the cost would decrease. Note, though: chickens attract rats, which are after the feed, and remember there's chicken poo to deal with too.

Some Facts about Buying Chickens

Before anything else, check with your local authority that you're allowed to keep livestock where you live. If you are and you want to go ahead:

- **You should get at least two** (a solitary chicken will not be happy). Between two and four hens will supply an average family.

- **As a guideline**, a hybrid hen produces about 300 eggs per year, or even as many as one a day. They live about four or five years.

- **Hybrids are best for producing eggs** because that's what they are bred for. Examples of hybrid breeds are Black Rock, ISA Brown, White Star and Loman. Hybrid chickens are pretty low-maintenance and easy to keep. They cost between £8 and £12 each. Pedigrees cost more and lay fewer eggs (people have them because they look pretty).

- **Chickens need to be immunized** against various diseases (they should come immunized).

- **Ideally you buy them** when they are between sixteen and twenty weeks old.

- **Buy online**, or check out local ads, vets, farmers, etc. There is loads of advice online.

- **You need a space at least approx. 2 x 1.33m** for your hen coop (including nesting area and run). It's best if you can let them out of the coop to run around the garden from time to time as well. However, if left to roam free they are likely to cause damage – they are jungle animals at heart and love foraging and hiding – so you will need to protect precious plants and flowers.

● **If you are a little bit handy**, you can make a chicken coop yourself. Chickens basically need a 'house' with a shelter to sleep in and sufficient nesting boxes, and a secure run where they can stretch their legs. Take into account the risk of predators: i.e. foxes, badgers and rats. In other words, the coop needs to be secure.

● **Chickens must be looked after** and cleaned out regularly.

● **Chickens eat pellets or mash** (a kind of chicken feed), which you can buy from local suppliers. You can feed them some scraps like bread, bits of veg, etc., but you should avoid giving them salty, sugary or fatty foods.

● **They need fresh water every day.**

● **Grit is essential** for chickens as they need to eat it to help their digestion. Either they can find it themselves when roaming around or you need to supply it for them.

● **They need bedding**: straw or dust-free wood shavings or leaves.

Bees

And, while we're at it, bees. I won't pretend I've turned beekeeper in the name of research, but again, a lot of townies keep bees on their roof, rather amazingly. (By the way, if you suffer from hay fever, eating locally produced honey can have miraculous results, as my son discovered years ago when we lived in east London and I spooned Hackney honey down him). Anyway, if you like the idea of having a little hive, and making money out of selling the results, have a look at the British Beekeepers' Association's website at www.britishbee.org.uk.

There is more on food scattered through some of the following chapters – use the index if you're after anything specific.

What Not to Scrimp On

Despite the money-saving ethos of this book, there are some things that are, I'm afraid, just cheap and nasty, and where the pennies saved don't even begin to make up for the loss of pleasure. In this chapter, in my opinion, those things would be butter and fresh coffee. There is no such thing as delicious cheap butter (unless you've found a glut of cream and made your own, as instructed above), and nor is there such a thing as a bag of fantastic coffee beans for 99p. You're just going to have to cough up. I also feel that cheap loo paper is really, really horrible, but maybe that's just me. To this small list, I would add organic meat and eggs. The idea of battery hens makes me want to be sick – in fact, I can't believe it's still legal to keep living creatures in such appalling conditions, let alone that people exist who feel fine about eating them, or their eggs. This is Hugh Fearnley-Whittingstall territory – have a look at his website, www.rivercottage.net (nice bunch of seasonal recipes on there too). If you are keen on keeping chickens or hens, as above, you can adopt rescued battery hens via the Battery Hen Welfare Trust, whose website is at www.bhwt.org.uk.

I **hate cheap clothes.** Well, no, that's not entirely true. There are, happily for this chapter, some cheap clothes I absolutely love, and I know for a fact that it is entirely possible to look like a million dollars on about thirty quid, if you're judicious. But I hate the high street stores that sell very cheap clothes, and the very cheap clothes they sell.

How do we think it became possible for a new dress to cost £6? If the finished garment, including the store's mark-up, costs £6, what do we think the person who made it was paid? What kind of conditions do we imagine they were working under? And how old do we think they were? Now, I like clothes and I like a bargain. But really, who could wear these clothes and feel good about it? (Answer: millions of punters. I find this insanely depressing. *And* they still look like crap.)

Wearing these clothes is basically saying, 'Yeah, I know, a broken, desperate eight-year-old girl who's paid 20p a week probably had a hand in the manufacturing of my dress, but never mind, because it was so cheap. Look, isn't it pretty?' Pretty isn't the word I'd use myself. I wonder what people who shop at those stores do on Red Nose Day, or other charity-friendly occasions. Do they feel all sorry for the little foreign children and their shit lives, and dig deep?

That's my main objection. There are many others. One, it is
the easiest thing in the world to buy clothes simply because
they are cheap. We've all done it. The garment itself is
adequate rather than fabulous; its main merit is that it's
'a bargain'. So we run around the store, scooping up armfuls
of ridiculously cheap T-shirts – which will inevitably fall
apart by the third wash – and think to ourselves, 'Yes,
but never mind about that, because it's so cheap that at
that point I'll just throw it away and get another one.' Now,
I don't know – maybe I'm in a minority on this one. But to
me this is more decadent, more appalling, more completely
morally bankrupt than the grotesquely rich women who
buy couture, of which there are about 2,000 worldwide
and only 200 who buy regularly, compared to the tens
of millions who buy cheap trash with a clear conscience.

The world has finite resources. Human beings have the right not to
slave away for 2p because some thick bint in London thinks she'll buy
the cheap dress and chuck it when it breaks. I feel a rant coming on
and you've probably got the gist, so I'll stop right there and move on. No,
actually – one more thing: according to TRAID (Textile Recycling for Aid
and International Development), 900,000 tonnes of clothes and shoes
are thrown away in the UK each year, of which only 200,000 tonnes are
rescued for recycling. The rest goes to landfill.

You pays your money and you takes your choice.

The point about cheap new clothes from the high street – I'm talking in
terms of aesthetics now – is that they're never very nice. The main point
of them is their cheapness. Cheap new clothes look cheap. I can spot a
cheap new dress at a hundred paces: bad colour (cheap black is especially

bad – it's never black enough,* and it'll be even less black after you wash it); bad prints (always looks cheap); crappy finish – awful seams, weird sizing; horrible fabrics – thin, cheap cotton that won't last the month, or static-giving, sweat-making synthetics . . . You get the picture. And, by the way, all of this applies to bags too – cheap leather is cheap for a reason and that reason is never good. At the time of writing, the *Ecologist* magazine has a report about leather from Bangladesh and ill-health resulting from the tanning process. Inform yourself wherever possible.

The dress that makes you feel fantastic, and has been making you feel fantastic for the past five years every time you put it on, or the trousers that make you look like you're on stilts: are you telling me that they were cheap? Because I don't believe you. There is, as we all know, artistry involved in making clothes. It's why Yves Saint Laurent was Yves Saint Laurent, and the person who knitted Gyles Brandreth's sweaters wasn't (and, by the way, I'm not exonerating high-end designers when I rant about evil cheap clothes: some of them use the same factories as the high street.† Always ask, and make a fuss if you don't like the answer you get, or if you're fobbed off with something vague. Don't be fobbed off. This is a real problem, and sooner or later we will all have to deal with the consequences. You may also want to have a read of Labour Behind the Label's 2007 report, 'Let's Clean Up Fashion', which you can find at www.labourbehindthelabel.org/resources).

---

* *Unlike cheap black hair dye, which is always too black and makes you look like some strangely matt crows died on your head. If you have black hair and want to cover the grey, always go lighter, unless you are a Goth. See pages 202–7.*

† *Just as some very 'grotty' supermarkets use the same factories to make their ready-meals as some very 'posh' ones.*

Shop the High Street with a Clear Conscience

The following stores have all explicitly stated their opposition to child labour. *

Marks & Spencer

'As we are 100 per cent own-brand we have great control over our supply chain. We know and audit all the factories we source from. These audits check that our standards are being met, which include: no child labour, no forced labour, no unauthorized subcontracting, workers must be paid at least the local minimum wage, and all overtime is paid and voluntary.'

American Apparel

'Clothing manufacturing is a very tough job, but we have always tried to do things differently . . . It comes down to this: not blindly outsourcing, but rather knowing the faces of our workers and providing them with the opportunity to make a fair wage. The average sewer with experience at American Apparel is making about $25,000/yr [£12,500] (i.e. $12/hr [£6], well over twice the federal minimum). This can be higher in some cases . . . we guarantee job security and full-time employment; this is an anomaly in the garment industry, which historically has been dominated by seasonal work.'

H&M

'We say no to child labour. As a business we have a responsibility to the employees of our suppliers. H&M does not own any of the factories that manufacture our products. We work with around 800 suppliers, mainly in Asia and Europe.'

* Source: © Lisa Armstrong, The Times, June 2008, NI Syndication

Arcadia Group (includes Topshop, Burton, Miss Selfridge, Wallis, Dorothy Perkins)

'We make it clear at the beginning of our relationship with a supplier that we will not work with any factory that employs children. To work with us, suppliers must agree to employ workers who meet the minimum legal age requirement in that country or the minimum age in our code, whichever is higher. We support the principle of a living wage. In 2007 we established the Fashion Footprint Group to align our social responsibilities with those of our business activities.'

Gap

'We do not own any of the factories that we buy from. If a factory chooses to subcontract or outsource any production, we insist that it also adheres to our code of conduct, which includes the prohibition of child labour, adherence to local labour laws, assurance of workers' freedom of association and no forced labour.'

Adili.com

'All the products Adili stocks tackle at least one of the environmental and social issues involved in making, transporting and selling clothes. We assess the brand and the product against ethical frameworks covering environmental impact, working conditions and fair trade. These cover the whole supply chain for a product.'

People Tree

'We are a very active member of IFAT, the International Fair Trade Association. We support 50 Fair Trade producer groups in 15 developing countries.'

The good news is, there exist more than enough gorgeous, well-made cheap clothes to go round – you just need to know where to look. But the very first thing I would say, counter-intuitively (yes, I know, it's supposed to be a book about *thrift*), is: when it comes to clothes, always buy the best you can afford. Spend as much money as you are able to, only don't do it very often – like, once or twice a year, not every Saturday. One fantastically cut, top-quality coat will last you upwards of ten years. A classic little black dress can last decades – and will be nicked by your daughter and fought over by your female grandchildren. A cashmere jumper is chic, warm, durable and beyond fashion. Good underwear can shave off 10lb, which I call entirely quidsworth (check old-lady-style underwear shops for old-fashioned girdles – much cheaper than miracle pants and just as effective. Also, can be curiously sexy, in a reinforced-nylon-gusset kind of way). Spend as much as you can on classic pieces. And:

Look after your clothes. This sounds obvious, but it's a lost art. Even good-quality clothes need a little help.

Stuff shoes or boots with crumpled-up newspaper to help them keep their shape between wears.

Learn to mend. Sew the dangling button back on to the dress lovingly and carefully. Ask someone to show you how to darn or patch a hole or tear. Keep an eye on your hems. Learn to take stuff in or, more probably, let stuff out.

Always use weather-proofing spray on anything made of suede, and on especially precious shoes and bags – it will prolong the item's life dramatically.

Learn to hand-wash (and see page 92 for various myths about the importance, so called, of dry-cleaning).

Get zips replaced, or learn to do it yourself.

 Learn to iron really well and use spray starch where appropriate. Old clothes often appear to be old because they're sort of floppy and tired-looking – you can stiffen them up again in minutes so they regain their jauntiness. Cheap corsages – fabric flowers – can also be de-drooped with spray starch.

Moth-proof your closets. Even if you don't have moths, you will. Those bastard moths get everywhere and can destroy your wardrobe.

Use a clothes brush, both to combat fluff and to keep fibres perky – this applies especially to winter coats and jackets, which can go a bit flat and shiny over the years if you don't.

Shave the bobbles off any woollen items regularly. Better still, buy posh ones – they bobble a great deal less, if at all.

Use really good deodorant, preferably unscented. Some of the more aggressive brands out there literally eat away at the fabric under your armpits (I don't even know why they exist: another example of women being made to feel paranoid about potential body 'issues'. Nobody sweats that much, unless they're an athlete).

Wear opaques, fishnets or bare legs (with fake tan where necessary). Thin tights just die after a couple of wears and are a complete waste of money, plus they look matronly.

Feed your leather handbags with specialist cleaner.

The Sales

It follows that, if you're going to be investing in expensive classics, the sales are a very good place to start. I wrote in **The Shops** about how I despised sales – all the stuff nobody wanted all year, just for you – but I am prepared to make an exception for everlasting, classic pieces, which are seasonless. The crucial thing about sales shopping, as with all bargain hunting, is not to get swayed into believing that something is nice simply because it is discounted. It is discounted for a reason, and the total must-have hotness of the item in question is never it. However, fashion houses do have to clear out their stock every now and then, and if the stock is reliably good, then it is indeed possible to pick up a bargain. Watch the sales like a hawk and attend them with single-minded devotion. If you have your eye on a black cashmere coat, don't get distracted and buy armfuls of last summer's maxi-dress just because they seem insanely cheap. They're insanely cheap because they're over.

The first day of the sales may yield some bargains, but the last will yield better ones – and remember that the bigger shops often put out new stock every day. It is worth signing up for some of the bigger stores' account cards – even if you don't actually ever use the card to shop and even though this is a mild hassle – because they often have sale previews for favoured customers (in London, Liberty's are legendary) and these are by far the most civilized way of bagging yourself a bargain. So do fill in the annoying little form by the till, because it'll come in handy one day. Your other option is to be told every time there is a designer sale – in London, this happens about once a month. Sign up to www.dailycandy.com and you'll get a free daily email telling you about cool new stuff, from shops (resist!) to restaurants (ditto), and including a slew of useful information about upcoming designer sales, where you can pick up incredible bargains.

Spend as little as you can on fashion with a sell-by-date. Better still, ignore fashion with a sell-by date altogether. I do, but then I'm middle-aged. I am still incredibly devoted to clothes, but I buy stuff because I like it and because it's flattering, not because a woman's magazine has told me it's this season's must-have – and I wear the stuff I like for years, if not decades. A classic, knitted silk Diane Von Furstenberg wrap dress, for instance, won't – unlike cheaper imitations – ever lose its shape, or bag, or sag, or fray, or gape, or start looking mumsy or past it. It'll cost you upwards of £200, yes, but you can wear it for twenty years (always do the maths: £200 dress over twenty years = £10 a year if you only wear it once a year. If you wear it once a month, it'll cost you 83p per wear). That's what I call a bargain. And I do think it pays (literally) to take the long view when it comes to clothes. The blah nylony dress that cost £40 and that you wear once works out far more expensive than the Vivienne Westwood number that you saved up for for six months but that makes you feel like a goddess – even when you're having a fat day, even when you're premenstrual, even when your hair looks really weird and you can't do anything about it – on any given day over any given decade. And remember, if something is just too expensive for comfort, there's always the shared purchase, where you split cost and ownership with a friend. This doesn't work if you need a new winter coat, but it does work if we're talking party frock.

Ultra-trendy clothes date, literally within months, sometimes weeks. Buy, if you must, one or two seasonal items from the ethical end of the high street, or better still buy cheap (but not cheap-looking) accessories instead. This is, incidentally, how people who work in fashion dress: not designers themselves (they tend to wear jeans), and not yer actual fashion editor, who has freebies and discount cards at her disposal, but the fashion assistants and junior stylists and girls who passionately love fashion but who have piddly salaries. It's always the same look: classic, with killer accessories, and one or two well-sourced high street versions of this season's must-have shape or style or colour. These people, by the way – I know a few – pore over pictures of Celeb X or Y, who the Great British Public absolutely idolize and wish they looked like, and die laughing. (They also always look affluent, even when you know for a fact that they're not. You know the sort of rich look, that patina of wealth some people just have, that lustre, even if they're wearing jeans and a T-shirt, and some people, try as they might to dip themselves in top-to-toe designer clothes, never seem to be able to muster? That's what you need to work on, more than the clothes. It's basically about skin, hair and teeth, but I'll go into it in more detail in the chapter on Beauty.)

So that is my first tip. Shop rarely, and buy a very little of the very best – but only classics. Spending a lot on this season's look is a waste of money.

On to the more classical version of thrift. First, read the blogs. There are hundreds, many of them US-centric but nevertheless useful and filled with good tips. Here are a few to get you started:

www.flatbrokefabulous.blogspot.com
Cheap inspiration from a cool fashion student.

www.thrillsandfrills.blogspot.com
Not a thrift blog per se, but nice writing, nice clothes and ingenious high street buys.

www.makedostyle.blogspot.com

It's called Make Do and Mend and it's about style on a budget, written by a stylist.

www.thebudgetbabe.com

Spots the trend, shows you how to get them cheaper.

http://brokeandbeautiful.com

So does she, plus she links to many other budget sites.

http://fdiary.wordpress.com

Budget Chic - confessions of a fashion cheapskate.

www.economyofstyle.blogspot.com

Cheerful and opinionated — how one woman squares her pash for fash with her mini wallet.

How to Shop from the US Without Leaving Your Home

Here is a very handy tip indeed if these blogs, or any of the US online stores, whet your appetite. Many of them don't ship outside of North America. So you're stymied. Except, not. This is what you do: go to www.myus.com and get yourself an account (not free, but worth it). What this company does is provide you with an American address, which you use when you're buying from US websites. They then forward your purchases to you at your UK address, whether they're clothes, books, rugs or furniture. Dead simple and dead ingenious, especially as there are incredible bargains to be had from US online shops – but, of course, if the nice shoes cost £5, please check they are ethically produced.

eBay

After that, eBay is your first port of call, obviously. One person's calamitous disaster is another's figure-perfecting dream. Some random tips – just a few of them, because we all know how to use eBay by now, I assume:

- **If you buy something from the same buyer more than once**, mark them as a favourite and keep an eye on their stock – if your tastes coincide, chances are there's plenty more to come. When I lost a load of weight and sold off my entire wardrobe, pretty much everything was bought by the same three people.

- **Don't be put off if the seller is abroad**, but check postage and packing costs. Some of my best bargains have come from the US – especially with the weakened dollar.

- **Investigate eBay 'boutiques' as well as individual buyers**. Some people are brilliant at making clothes but don't have the money to open up a real bricks-and-mortar shop, so they have cyber ones instead. Take a look at www.etsy.com, of which much more later (see the next chapter). It is absolutely packed with amazing, original clothes, made by highly talented 'normal' people rather than designers, at some very bargainous prices. Plus, you develop a relationship with the seller, so that having the odd thing customized – made longer, or with a frill, or whatever – may become a possibility.

- **Always ask what the returns policy is before bidding**. A good seller should take the item back and refund you without quibbling if the garment is for any reason inappropriate.

- **Don't be discouraged by marks or small tears** – they're fixable (and they usually bump down the price). This applies especially to vintage.

- **Do use a sniper** – very annoying for everybody else, but essential if you really want something and can't be in front of the computer as the auction ends. Try www.auctionsniper.com – the idea is that this automatically monitors the sale and leaps in during the last minutes (or seconds) with a winning bid, even if all it takes to secure a winning bid is an extra 20p.

- **Beware of imitations**, unless you are specifically in search of designer knock-offs. It is much wiser and more gratifying to look for vintage Ossie Clarke than for this season's Louis Vuitton, which is more than likely to be a fake.

Swapping

The thing about eBay is that it can be quite time-consuming. The beauty of swapping is that you do it in one night, among friends, with wine and chat (but not keys – I'm making it sound like *échangisme*). Clothes swaps are all the rage, and no wonder: they're fun, free, and they make perfect sense. You can swap online, go to an event or organize your own swapping parties with your friends (make sure several of you are the same dress size, otherwise it doesn't work).

Have a look at some of these websites for inspiration. They're only the tip of a vast iceberg:

Online Swaps

www.whatsmineisyours.com

Buy and swap (or barter for) designer clothing, vintage clothing and high street fashion.

www.rehashclothes.com

Swap clothes, accessories and books, make friends and help the environment.

www.swapstyle.com

Describes itself as 'the world's biggest online fashion party'. Swap clothes, accessories, cosmetics, shoes and more.

www.swishing.org

Fashion swapping parties.

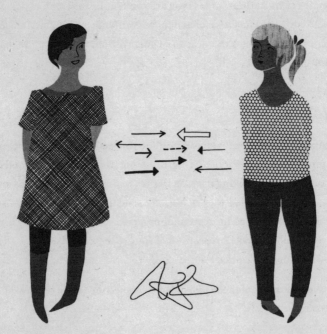

Public Events

~ *www.swaporamarama.org*

A terrific American site which organizes not only clothes swap
parties but also things like sewing workshops alongside, so
you can learn how to customize your clothes. At the time of
writing, there was a Swap-o-Rama-Rama event in Brighton,
so here's hoping the idea takes off in the rest of the UK.

~ *www.myspace.com/swaparamarazzmatazz*

Swapping parties held monthly at (currently) Favela Chic, 91–93
Great Eastern Street, London EC2A 3HZ; tel: 020 7613 4228.

Hold a Party Yourself

It's not rocket science – you pick a night, ask your friends, and ask
them to bring their friends, make sure everyone has more than one
person to swap with size-wise, get some wine in, and away you go.

Here are some tips:

~ **Make sure the clothes on offer are freshly laundered.**

~ **Don't be too picky about what you bring to swap.**
You'd be surprised what people want – one man's trash, etc.

~ **Make sure you have enough space** for people to rummage around
and try things on – you don't want anyone tripping over the dog.

~ **Have at least two full-length mirrors on hand.**

~ **Work out before you begin what you will do in the event of two
people wanting the same item.** Tossing a coin is always good, or
you could suggest that the two people involved do a mini catwalk
strut and everyone else votes on who the item suits best.

Customizing and Refashioning Clothes

This is really worth doing – it can revitalize your entire wardrobe, especially the stuff you are too emotionally attached to to get rid of but are nevertheless reluctant to wear. You can learn to love it by:

- **Altering clothes so that they fit impeccably**. If you don't feel confident enough to do this yourself (though see page 83), take the item to the dry-cleaner's or to a tailor, should you be lucky enough to know of such a thing – it's still cheaper than buying a new frock. I rely on people working in the windows of dry-cleaner's in grotty areas – that sounds a bit blunt, but there's no point in going to the poshest one in the poshest area. Also look online and in the back of your local newspapers for seamstresses – there are often people who are brilliant at sewing and work from home for extra money.

- **Turning them into something that you will wear**. This requires some creative thinking and some basic sewing skills, but see the websites below. For instance, when I had the moth, rather than throw away half my dresses, I chopped them off just above the moth holes, hemmed them and, voila, slightly shorter/sleeveless versions of my old favourites given an instant new twist.

- **Changing the buttons and/or the trimming**. Mother of pearl buttons, or whatever kind you like, make everything a great deal more exciting, and typically you only need four or six buttons, so it's cheap. An old cardi can be transformed by an organdie trim or a bit of judicious ribbon.

- **Chopping up old T-shirts and giving them new necklines**. I used to do this all the time in the 1980s and have recently started doing it again, because I can never find T-shirts with flattering necklines. No need to hem or sew – all you need are some sharp scissors. The finished result is manageably edgy: i.e. cool-looking without being bonkers.

- **Finding a local haberdashery and using it wisely**. It will supply you with expensive-looking trimmings, corsages, feathers, fake flowers, sequins – all the stuff you need to turn a blah high street dress into a hot little number. In London, try VV Rouleaux (www.vvrouleaux.com) for a selection of exquisite ribbons and trimmings.

- **Polishing your shoes**. Obvious, but makes a huge difference. And don't buy new ones: make use of your cobbler and get things reheeled. A good cobbler can also stretch shoes and boots so that they stop giving you blisters/making your calves look bulgy (if they're really bulgy, try www.duoboots.com and www.vivaladiva.com for good styles in wide calf fittings). They can also mend, or even dye, that expensive handbag you used to love (and please don't buy expensive high-fashion handbags: the It bag is dead, anyway, and it ages incredibly badly). If you're in London, Classic Shoes (23–25 Brecknock Road, London N7 0BL: tel: 020 7485 5275) is the best there is – every single high-end shoe designer uses them. They can perform miracles, plus it's a family business and they're lovely. (By the way, if you like these location-specific tips, which I'm not doing too many of at the risk of becoming useless to anyone who doesn't live in London, check out and contribute to www.tipped. co.uk and http://trustedplaces.com – both are online nationwide communities of people tipping other people about their great finds).

- **Turning stuff that really can't be reinvented into cushions**. You don't even need a sewing machine, and old jumpers make lovely cosy ones. Fab prints adorning dresses that are simply past it can make stunning cushions also. I love www.recycle-eh.com/textiles.htm, because the woman who writes it isn't very good at sewing and doesn't let it deter her. She doesn't stop at cushions either: tea cosies, soft toys, felted purses and hats, hot-water bottles . . . Look at the website for brilliant information and see the next chapter for a great deal more on crafting.

Following the example of a movement in the US called Wardrobe Refashion, where people pledge to not buy any new clothes and instead to refashion or make their own clothes for a certain amount of time. There are dozens of blogs related to this, and lots of people coming up with lots of good ideas and tips – just Google it. Have a look here to get started: http://nikkishell.typepad.com/wardroberefashion. Then maybe go here: www.sweetsassafras.org/category/sewing.

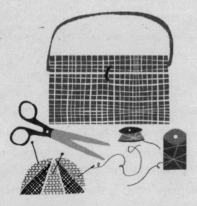

Using dye. When I still used to go to a French school (in London), which is to say when my English wasn't great, we used to drive past a certain dry-cleaner's in Baker Street every morning. They had a big sign in their window saying WE WILL DYE FOR YOU. I thought it was the most ingenious wordplay I'd ever seen and marvelled at it every day. The dry-cleaner's is still there; a few months ago, as we were driving past, one of my children said, 'WE WILL DYE FOR YOU – that's quite clever,'

which immediately took me back to being ten or eleven. Anyway, as I was saying, dyeing stuff. Cold-water dyeing just needs a bucket and some salt; doing it in the washing machine is even easier. Dyeing works best on natural fabrics (synthetics dye too, but you can't be as sure of the colour – pink can go purple and so on, depending on the material). It is completely marvellous for rejuvenating grotty-looking underwear – from grubby grey-white to vermilion, from that horrible 'natural' colour to turquoise – but also for T-shirts, old shirts, socks – anything, really. Old white towels past their prime respond especially well.

Sewing, which has become incredibly cool, especially if you're under thirty. If, like me, the only sewing you've ever done was decades ago at school and you think of it as a nice hobby for grannies, think again. (This is also true of knitting, crochet and crafts in general, which is why there's a whole chapter on this subject coming up next.) It shouldn't be too difficult to find a sewing class near you via your local authority, or via our trusty friend Google. Chances are you'll not only learn something useful but meet some great people too. Which leads us neatly to . . .

Sewing Your Own Clothes

If you're a sewing virgin, or haven't sewn since school, you're going to have to take my word on this one: sewing is quite easy, unless you want to make a ball gown or a wedding dress. It is also amazingly economical and fun, and provides the most enormous sense of satisfaction. All you need is a sewing machine, a pattern and some fabric. It is brilliantly useful if you are an 'unusual' size or shape and find that shop-bought clothes don't fit you especially well. Once you've learned the basics, you will get the confidence to fiddle with and adapt patterns until everything you make looks made-to-measure, which indeed it will be. Plus, your clothes will be original, cheap and beautiful. Stuff that in your pipe, Primark.

Before you start off, take a look at www.threadbanger.com for inspiration. It's a site of genius and will start you off in whatever direction you want to take, from making a denim skirt out of an old pair of jeans to making fairy wings.

The first thing to do is to familiarize yourself with the whole sewing-machine scenario. Do this before you buy a machine. The John Lewis group (branches nationwide, see www.johnlewis.com for details of your nearest one) has especially impressive sewing/haberdashery departments, staffed by really knowledgeable people who seem infinitely patient and kind. They also run brilliant 'learn to use a sewing machine' sessions. So sign up for a sewing class or join a sewing circle. Try your local community centre, sewing shop or yarn shop, or even school noticeboard for details of local beginners' courses. And remember, we may not be good at sewing, but previous generations were, and still are. Ask your mum, your granny, your aunties, that nice older lady who lives down the road to show you how.

Once you're sufficiently enthused/confident, don't go mad and buy a top of the range machine. You can buy a new, lightweight and easy to use machine that'll cater to basic dressmaking needs for around £100. All you need it to be able to do is straight stitch and zigzag stitch. Unless you're planning to take this up professionally, it makes sense to split the cost with a couple of like-minded friends – it's more fun, too, to have each other's help and input, and we're talking £33 each for the foundations for a whole new wardrobe.

Take your shoes off when using the machine – the pedals are very sensitive and you get a lot more control if you can feel how much pressure you're applying. Go really, really slowly.

Start with something simple, such as a square bag or a cushion cover. Or customize a T-shirt. When you evolve on to a basic dress or skirt, think about fabric: the basic rule is measure twice, cut once. This is important, as I found out the hard way.

A basic dress or skirt, you're thinking. BUT HOW? Websites can give you much better information here than I can, because they show you as well as tell you. Try:

- *http://howtomakeclothes.wordpress.com*
- *www.threadbanger.com* (has videos)
- *www.sewmamasew.com*
- *www.craftster.org*
- *www.videojug.com*

There are literally hundreds of others – the 'links' sections of the ones I've mentioned will lead you to them.

Keep going. When you've completed your first project, start another one. Practice makes perfect.

Fabric

With fabric, stick to basic initially – that means non-slippery and not too textured. Use cotton thread for cotton, synthetic for anything else. Fabric can be expensive in the UK but check out John Lewis or your local haberdashery in the first instance. In London, MacCulloch & Wallis (www.macculloch-wallis.co.uk) is great and very reasonable, while the Cloth House (www.clothhouse.com) is divine but expensive.

It can be cheaper to buy your fabric from the US online but watch out for shipping costs. Try the following:

www.reprodepotfabrics.com
For vintage reproduction and retro fabrics, quirky buttons, ribbons and sewing patterns.

www.purlsoho.com
For the most glorious selection of fabrics and accessories.

www.equilter.com
For an amazing array of fabrics and a helpful 'design board' that allows you to play with thumbnail photos of fabrics.

www.superbuzzy.com
For some very cute Japanese fabrics.

Patterns

New patterns cost about £8 each, but you can buy them cheap via eBay and there are lots available free online: try www.burdastyle.com. Have a look at www.debsrecycledsewingpatterns.com for inspiration. Vintage patterns (not free) are available from, among a slew of others: www.etsy.com, www.borntoolatevintage.com and www.misshelene.com.

Patterns are graded by difficulty, so don't ignore the grades if you're a novice. And buy a pattern in your size – don't think, 'Oh poo, they only have it in a size 10, but I'll just bump the measurements down/up and be fine.' Not if you're new to this, you won't.

Vintage

If that all sounds a bit scary, then there's always vintage, which we rather less glamorously used to call second-hand. Here's how to track down the best stuff:

Travel to charity shops in posh areas if you're after designer cast-offs or, more interestingly, the kinds of clothes (or costume jewellery) rich old ladies might be discarding.

Be thorough. People have their charities of choice, which means that in one neighbourhood Oxfam may yield nothing but Marie Curie might be a treasure trove, or vice versa. If you're trawling the charity shops, trawl all of them.

If you've got the sewing bug, remember that you can adapt most things. If you're mad about the fabric but not the cut, and if the item's cheap enough, think laterally: it may make a brilliant skirt, or great cushion covers (I think I'm sounding a bit obsessed with these. That's because I am. So quick! So easy! So pretty! Make such nice presents!).

Have a look in charity shops wherever you are. Sometimes the most unpromising-seeming tiny village shop has brilliant gems, while the giant metropolitan one doesn't. I once found a whole trove of original Welsh blankets in a Welsh charity shop in the middle of nowhere, and an amazing original Halston dress in, of all places, Moreton-in-Marsh. Rural tastes don't necessarily coincide with urban ones — make this work in your favour.

Always check out market stalls, even if you're thinking, 'But this market is for sixteen-year-old Goths and German teenagers.' You'd be surprised. It's all to do with having the time and patience to look through every rail.

Don't dismiss the big vintage emporia – such as Beyond Retro in London (www.beyondretro.com) – on the basis that they've marked everything up and stopped it being a bargain. The goodness of stores such as these is that they have sharply edited collections, which save a huge amount of time and stop you having to wade through piles of dross (and German teenagers) to find the jewel. And the clothes are still a fraction of the price you'd pay for new. *Sehr gut!*

Ask (politely) if you can have a look through your friends' mums' or grannies' attics. I know women in their sixties and seventies who have incredible, perfectly preserved clothes that they don't wear any more and don't quite know what to do with. I was talking to an older friend when Celia Birtwell was doing a mini collection for Topshop which practically caused riots. 'Didn't she used to be married to Ossie Clarke?' my friend said innocently. 'I have masses of that stuff upstairs.' Give the clothes a happy home, but always offer to pay, and be insistent about it when you're initially dismissed with a polite 'no, no'.

Don't just shop for vintage clothes – check out shoes, bags and accessories. Vintage jewellery just rocks ass.

Go to every car boot sale and church fair in your neighbourhood – www.carbootsrus.com will list them all (and see pages 131–2 for a list of my favourites). Better still, organize one yourself and get first dibs. A better wardrobe and you raise funds for charity – what's not to love?

Older clothes tend to be better made, by which I mean also made of more fabric. If you're a size 12 and the 10 fits, but in a sausage-skin way, check out the seams. Chances are there's spare fabric to let the garment out.

Speaking of which, try everything on – don't rely on the label. Sizing has changed wildly in the past few decades to accommodate women's increasing bigness (I don't mean fatness, I mean bigger chests, thicker waists and so on), as well as increasing vanity.

Beware of buying stuff that will make you look like you're going to a fancy-dress party. I love 1940s dresses, for instance, but some of them can make you look a bit Joan Crawford, especially if you're as devoted to the eyebrow as I am. Again, always try before you buy.

Befriend the owners of your favourite, most-frequented shops. Good ones with whom you have built up a relationship over the months or years will put stuff aside for you – this is especially useful if you're an 'unusual' size or shape. If you're going to do this, don't go shopping wearing a tracksuit, but wear the kind of clothes you'd like to have more of, so they get an idea of what you like.

 Talk to the shop people. There's usually stuff in the back that hasn't been sorted, labelled or priced yet. Be specific about what you want and are looking for.

Always check armpits for staining (nice) or wear and tear, especially if the fabric is delicate.

Mix it up. Wearing top-to-toe vintage is quite tricky to pull off unless you have a strong sense of your own style, or like dressing in period fashion (there's a nice menstrual-sounding phrase).

The online vintage stores are getting better and better. My absolute favourite is www.legacy-nyc.com – a small but ever-changing selection of serious fashion and accessories (this is where you come for your vintage Hermès bag), brilliantly edited by the splendid Rita Brookoff, who also sells the most fantastic new vintage-style dresses (in amazing vintage prints) under her own label, Legacy. Not especially cheap, though rock-bottom compared to buying these pieces first-hand, and the weedy dollar really helps. She'll post stuff worldwide. I'm also mad about What Comes Around Goes Around, whose website is www.nyvintage.com. This is a larger organization, but their stuff is, again, brilliantly edited. They'll also ship worldwide. Needless to say, both have bricks-and-mortar shops in Manhattan and are very much worth the detour (they're round the corner from each other) if you're in New York. There are hundreds of online vintage shops in the UK too – try www.absolutevintage.co.uk, www.fuk.co.uk and www.marthascloset.co.uk.

Remember, you can ask shop owners with whom you have built up a relationship to try and source specific stuff for you. Obviously, don't walk into a random store and demand that they find you 1930s tea dresses in impeccable condition, because they'll think you're rude and mad. But once you've got to know each other – and once you've shown you're serious by buying stuff – it's always worth a try.

Don't forget to sell your own stuff: one of the many beauties of the Internet is that everyone can become a vintage dealer – and what you're bored with or no longer like is bound to be right up somebody else's alley. Use eBay, or check out sites such as www.fashiondig.com for inspiration. Note that American customers are totally anal about stuff coming from 'smoke-free homes'.

My dear (and visionary) old friend Orsola de Castro has been making and selling the most fabulous clothes, all of which are entirely recycled – i.e. made of bits of other clothes – since 1997, under the label From Somewhere, www.fromsomewhere.co.uk. I can't recommend them highly enough. Not cheap, but beautiful.

Selling Your Clothes on eBay

If you buy vintage and it doesn't fit, or you realize that that 1980s cocktail dress is a bit too **Dallas**, you can just sell it on again via eBay. This can be time-consuming if you're only selling bits and pieces and not making a business out of it, but it really couldn't be easier and it's actually quite fun to watch people fighting over your things.

There are really clear selling instructions on eBay but here are some general tips:

 Set up a PayPal account (www.paypal.com). PayPal is a completely safe and brilliant way of transferring money via the Internet that works just like a bank account: buyers deposit their payment in your PayPal account and you then transfer the money into your current account. If you don't transfer the money into your current account, it's actually a really good way to save up for something you want to buy online.

 Before you begin setting up your listing, search for similar items of clothing that are already listed to get an idea of what you should write and how low you should start your auction.

A picture is key and preferably a picture of the item being modelled (by you or a friend) in good lighting.

Compose your listing title carefully, thinking about what you would search under if you were looking for this item. For example, 'vintage 1980s prom-style pink cocktail dress, size 8' has more chance than 'vintage pink dress'.

Make sure you include measurements (like armpit to armpit, shoulder to hem, waist to hem, inside leg, etc.) in your listing – bidders may be put off by having to ask questions.

Caring for Your Clothes

Finally, caring for all these lovely clothes. Here's what I think: that dry-cleaning is mostly a myth, and an exorbitant myth at that. Clothing manufacturers have to protect themselves against shrinkage, which is why they stick 'Dry Clean' labels in everything, willy-nilly, but the truth of the matter is, you can wash nearly everything by hand. I was sceptical about this when I was first told, by a friend with a dazzling wardrobe and a serious thrifty streak, but it turns out to be true. Here's the information:

Anything that has a label saying 'Dry Clean' can be washed by hand.

Anything that has a label saying 'Dry Clean ONLY' can probably still be washed by hand, but approach with caution. Anything that says 'Dry Clean Only' and is absolutely filthily stained goes to the dry-cleaner's, as serious stain-removing at home is risky (though possible – see www.ktcampbell.com/domesticity/hand_wash.html, among others).

The easy method, and the one to use on anything you're especially anxious about: go to the brilliant Lakeland, www.lakeland.co.uk, and spend £8.99 on their Hagerty® Dry-Cleaning Kit. This marvel will turn your tumble dryer into a dry-cleaning machine (which is really what a professional dry-cleaning machine is – a huge dryer plus some chemicals) and clean up to sixteen items. Use without fear – it's brilliant and it works, even on big things like coats, for 56p a pop at the time of writing.

The more nerve-racking but still completely effective method:

* Get some very mild soap, such as Dr Bronner's Castile Soap, available in liquid form from most health food shops. Dissolve some in hot water and then add cold so that the water is tepid.

* Rub dirty spots or marks very gently – like, with one finger, using a stroking motion. Vigorous rubbing buggers up the fibres and will ruin your garment.

* Swirl the clothes around the sink – don't do anything more energetic. If they're not stained, I don't even swirl. I just leave them sitting there in the warm soapy water for a bit. Never, ever twist, or scrub, or wring.

* Let out the soapy water and replace with clean, cold water. Swirl your clothes around until they are rinsed, changing the water as appropriate.

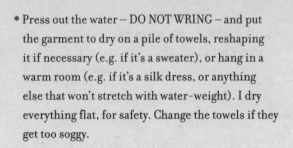

* Press out the water – DO NOT WRING – and put the garment to dry on a pile of towels, reshaping it if necessary (e.g. if it's a sweater), or hang in a warm room (e.g. if it's a silk dress, or anything else that won't stretch with water-weight). I dry everything flat, for safety. Change the towels if they get too soggy.

* Leave until dry (though see below for silk). This works beautifully for wool, including cashmere, and silk. Rayon is incredibly shrinky: don't even stroke or swirl it. Just dunk it and leave it for a few minutes.

For big items, such as winter coats, use the Lakeland wonder method.

Iron your sweaters lightly when dry – this stops them feeling stiff from contact with water. Iron silk when it's still slightly damp.

Having hand-washed an item, never, EVER stick it in the dryer. It will shrink to death.

American washing machines, unlike British ones, have very, very quick delicates programmes, some lasting mere minutes. Should you find yourself in the US with a suitcase full of dirty clothes, it is perfectly safe to ignore all of the above and stick your cashmeres and silks (with the appropriate – i.e. made-for-delicates – detergent) on the quickest programme of one of these machines (which are everywhere domestically, but also in some Laundromats).

What Not to Scrimp On

As I was saying above, long-lasting classics. And, if you need your underwear to modify your figure, then I implore you to check out the figure-altering, pounds-shrinking, modern version of 'control wear'. Leather (there is nothing sadder-looking than cheap leather). Some might add denim, but I'm not one of them – the whole £200 pair of jeans phenomenon (talk about marketing genius) completely passed me by. I wear Gap jeans, or ancient Levi's, and am very happy with them. Note: don't be tempted by cheaper-than-M&S cashmere: it pills and bobbles and wears badly. M&S's is excellent and durable.

Crafts

*I*f you're **under thirty and fairly with it**, you'll probably understand what I'm talking about when I say the craft movement is HUGE and super-cool. If you're over thirty, or you live in a hole (which is admirably thrifty of you), you may have no idea whatsoever of what I'm talking about, so here's a quick overview.

I'm not a craft historian, but as far as I am aware there are two points. One, some people have been crafting and knitting all along – many of our mothers' generation picked up the habit post-war and never gave it up. Two, running alongside was a newer, cooler underground movement which really kicked off on a massive scale in 2001, with the arrival, in America, of *ReadyMade* magazine, which is still going strong: see www.readymademag.com. This was a beautiful, hip, savvy, design-conscious magazine 'for people who like to make stuff'. It acknowledged the movement that already existed, as well as making it fashionable. A couple of years later, one Debbie Stoller wrote a seminal book called *Stitch 'n Bitch: The Knitter's Handbook* (Workman, £10.99), which sold 200,000 copies in the six months following publication and which, as its name makes explicit, reclaimed knitting from your granny's hobby to something cool, modern, creative and hip. The book, which is brilliant (and very much still in print), teaches even the most cack-handed knitter how to knit, with step-by-step instructions and illustrations, as well as providing desirable, sexy patterns for stuff you'd actually want to own.

Stoller founded the first Stitch 'n Bitch knitting group in New York; spin-offs followed in Chicago and Los Angeles (at which point, bewilderingly for the gossip magazines, photographs started appearing of hot young starlets knitting on set). It's no overstatement to say that Stoller's book, which was followed by three others, including an equally brilliant crochet book called *The Happy Hooker*, sparked off a worldwide phenomenon: S&B knitting groups now take place worldwide – you can find your nearest one at www.stitchnbitch.co.uk (there's more on knitting and knitting groups below). By the time *ReadyMade* magazine published its own book, crafts were so hip that people like Dave Eggers wrote blurbs for it.

The blogosphere went craft-crazy. Absolutely everyone was at it, it seemed, making things in a fun, cheerful, quirky, edgy, modern-seeming way. Part of the charm of the slew of craft blogs was, and remains, that the majority of these people were self-taught, so that, reading them, you got the sense that you were all in it together, learning as you went, encouraging and helping each other. There was, it's fair to say, an absolute explosion of online creativity, with savvy young women reclaiming and often also reinventing every single 'traditional' craft you could possibly think of. They were making really, really nice things – and sharing their methods as they went, not just by blogging but by putting up videos on their own websites or on YouTube, by photographing their progress and, often, by writing with enviable verve and brio. They made jokes, which up until then was unheard of in the rather po-faced world of crafting. They even made fun of themselves. And they made really cool stuff. Not cool in a 'that's quite cool for a home-made thing' way but cool in an 'I want one now' kind of way.

I could write an entire book about all of this, and about what it means – wahey – for so many young women to be redefining domesticity in such empowering, self-sufficient ways. For our current purposes, though, all you need to know is that:

- **Crafts are hot.**

- **Crafts are cheap.**

- **Crafts are the best fun and intensely satisfying.**

- **Crafts can dress you.**

- **Crafts make brilliant presents.**

- **Crafts can be sold and make you money.**

There's never been a better time to get into crafting. There is literally a whole world of information and support out there. If I am whetting your appetite, your first port of call should probably be www.craftster. org, the granddaddy of them all and a site that contains everything about everything to do with crafts, as well as being a giant online community.

But let's try and break it down a bit. I suggest you start by reading some of the craft blogs. Both www.craftyblogs.co.uk and www.craftgossip. com attempt to list and categorize all of the good crafty stuff on the Internet, not entirely successfully. I will list some of my personal favourites, all of which have links that will lead you to hundreds more. Some of these are a mixture of crafts and cookery (there's huge overlap, obviously); many of them blog about their domestic life as well as their crafting. These blogs are bliss, like eating boiled eggs and soldiers while wearing cashmere slippers. They are also completely inspirational.

You'll notice that a few of the bloggers below have their own books out: publishers were rather slow at catching up with the new craft movement, but no longer. And some of them have their own online shops: do bear in mind that there is serious money to be made by crafting. (By the way, my advice to any aspirant writer these days, assuming they need to have a 'real' day job, is blog, blog, blog. The number of publishing contracts/newspaper columns and so on that come about as a result is phenomenal, plus writing in public in this way – with loads of feedback – is an excellent discipline if your ambitions lie in an authorly direction.)

Anyway, the blogs. Well, some of them, and in no particular order:

http://angrychicken.typepad.com
Contagiously enthusiastic, with fantastic sewing ideas for everyone, whether you're inexperienced or a pro (its author, Amy Karol, is also the author of a genius book called Bend the Rules Sewing, which I can't recommend highly enough).

http://rosylittlethings.typepad.com/posie_gets_cozy
Compellingly adorable blog featuring everything from crafts to recipes. Like having a warm bath.

www.yarnstorm.blogs.com
Jane Brocket's inspirational and dazzlingly beautiful blog. Amazing use of colour; likely to induce violent lifestyle envy.

http://apronthriftgirl.typepad.com
More of a general thrift blog this one.

http://makinggooduse.typepad.co.uk
Jaunty British blog about trying to be thrifty and green, with a big crafts emphasis.

http://weewonderfuls.typepad.com
Has free patterns for very cute projects: fabric or woollen dolls, bunnies, a particularly nice pig.

http://loobylu.com
Lovely blog that combines domesticity, family life, home decoration and crafting.

www.mollychicken.blogs.com/my_weblog
Another visually lovely blog with loads of inspirations on the craft and home fronts.

www.purlbee.com
Part of the wonderful yarn shop in New York; has brilliant free knitting patterns.

If you enjoy these, there are hundreds, if not thousands, more out there and they're easy to find by checking out the above websites' links.

Knitting (and Crochet)

First things first: explore the vast, friendly and authoritative www.knitty.com. It will inspire, intrigue and amuse you, and provide you with all the knitting information a human being could conceivably need. There are many smaller, super-friendly British sites — I especially like www.castoff.info and www.ukhandknitting.com.

Knitting enormous items — jumpers, cardigans, jackets — is incredibly satisfying. It is not especially economical compared to buying a machine-knitted, mass-produced sweater. But bear in mind that just off Bond Street, London, an admittedly beautiful but also chunky and clearly home-made jumper goes for upwards of £400. You could totally make one yourself. Add the not insignificant fact that you're peacefully sitting at home, fully engaged and being creative and self-sufficient, rather than running about town spending money and acquiring hangovers, and YOU'RE A WINNER. Knitting and crochet are extra-specially thrifty if you're talking small items, such as scarves, socks, baby clothes or dolls. It is also thrifty if you want to knit or crochet a scarf out of some seriously luxe yarn: even using cashmere will set you back a fraction of what you'd pay in the shops.

I've mentioned Debbie Stoller's excellent books, above (see pages 97–8), but really the very best way of all of learning how to knit is to physically be shown. You can check out knitting videos on a variety of websites, including (among many others) www.howcast.com and www.videojug.com, but I'd just head for www.knittinghelp.com, which is packed with them. YouTube is also crawling with how-to knitting and crochet (and craft generally) videos; just do a search.

Being shown online is great, but better still is being shown by your mum, your granny, your elderly neighbour or (quite probably) your twenty-something one. Ask around: you'd be surprised how many people knit. Failing that, join a knitting group – they're cool, friendly, can be a great laugh and provide wonderful (and free!) information, help and advice. The aforementioned www.stitchnbitch.co.uk is a good starting point, as is www.knitchicks.co.uk. If there isn't a group near you (unlikely, frankly), then start your own: making your own entertainment is not only commendably thrifty but a great deal more fun than sitting around waiting for non-boring things to take place. You could also join a knitting class, but I find they are expensive and not nearly as much fun or as interesting as knitting groups. Having said that, if you're a Londoner you might want to check out a couple of exceptions to the rule by visiting the glorious Loop (Islington), www.loop.gb.com, and/or IKnit (Waterloo), www.iknit.org.uk. There is also the most wonderful yarn/crafty shop in Whitstable, Kent, called Seaside Sadie (64 Harbour Street, Whitstable CT5 1BZ; tel: 07811 201229, open Fridays and weekends), which also runs felting classes and seems to be a shining example of how to turn your hobby into a life-enhancing part-time business. And check out your local evening classes too – they're inexpensive and offer up a whole world of information for the wannabe crafter (or the wannabe mechanic, for that matter, or the wannabe furniture maker. Very underrated thing, evening classes – cheap as chips and tremendously useful).

Yarn

What is rather odd, and sad, is that even as knitting/crocheting/crafting becomes the acme of cool, yarn shops are dying. You can find your nearest one, wherever you are in the world, at www.knitmap.com. Unless you're lucky enough to live near one, or near a John Lewis that has a haberdashery department (not all of them do, alas), or near a department store with a yarn section (in London Liberty is wonderful, plus it has a famously great knitting group), you'll have to buy online. This is easily done – the only thing you have to remember is that you need to bear dye lots in mind, rather as when you're buying wallpaper: yarn colour can vary if it's not all from the same batch. If you buy your yarn, start your project and find you need some more, make sure the extra yarn is from the same lot as the first one, otherwise things'll go wonky. Try some of these online suppliers:

- *www.angelyarns.com*

- *www.laughinghens.com*

- *www.loop.gb.com/shop.html*
  (or go to the real shop in Islington, it's heaven).

- *www.hipknits.co.uk*

- *www.designeryarns.uk.com* (for real shops as well as cyber ones).

- *www.considerthelily.co.uk*

- *www.mcadirect.com*

- *www.purlsoho.com* (in New York, it's amazing; will ship to the UK, which wouldn't be thrifty, but the store is so great I had to mention it).

- *www.fun2do.co.uk* (which sells a thing called a Knifty Knitter, a lightweight plastic knitting loom manufactured for children and beginners, that can make hats, scarves, socks and a really cool little woolly octopus, among other things; KKs also come up on eBay).

You can, of course, get free yarn by unravelling old sweaters (the bigger the better, unless you're after stripes), or by buying them cheap from charity shops for this purpose. There are comprehensive instructions on how to do this at www.az.com/~andrade/knit/thrifty.html and also at www.instructables.com/id/How-to-recycle-an-old-sweater-or-a-botched-one-i/.

As for patterns, you can buy them, of course, but the Internet is a great resource for free ones. Have a look at www.knittingpatterncentral.com, which is a great site, stuffed with information, tips and tutorials. See also www.knitknack.co.uk, and the aforementioned www.threadbanger.com, which is ostensibly about sewing but covers a vast range of topics, including How to Knit.

Patchwork and Quilting

Patchwork

Patchwork and quilting are two separate crafts, which combine in the form of patchwork quilts – it's a brilliant thing to do with odd, random little scraps of pretty fabric. Patchwork doesn't have to be geometrically pristine; it can be as chaotic as you please, as long as you like the finished result. It's also a very nice way of putting together significant bits of material: a bit of your baby's first bib, for instance, with a bit of christening outfit, with a bit of first school uniform, and so on. Or you could make a wedding patchwork, or remember your granny by patchworking bits of her old dresses, or an old beloved house by patchworking bits of old tablecloth, tea towel, curtain and the like . . . Or you could be less sentimental than I am (though these small random patchworks, framed, make brilliant and original presents, especially if you're commemorating an occasion) and just use normal scraps to put together something beautiful and useful and free. You can patchwork by hand or by sewing machine – you can do anything you like, really. The classic things to make are cushions, blankets or quilts, but use your imagination too. As ever, the web is crawling with tips, projects and inspiration. Here are a few pointers:

www.bean-sprouts.blogspot.com/2008/02/how-to-make-patchwork.html

http://lindamade.wordpress.com/2007/08/28/
  hot-stuff-patchwork-oven-mitts

*www.creativelittledaisy.typepad.com/photos/purses_arent_the_only_*
  thi/babyquilt.html
Pictures of patchwork blankets, cushions, quilts, etc. for inspiration.

www.designspongeonline.com/2008/04/diy-project-janes-patchwork-
  chair.html
Fabulous project from one of the best design blogs (see Home chapter for more of these).

www.greenkitchen.com/blog/2007/06/stripe-y-patchwork-cat-front

See pages 85–6 for some good fabric suppliers and also try:
www.pelennapatchworks.co.uk and, as ever, the glorious *www.purlsoho.com* for quilting and patchwork tools and accessories.

Quilting

Quilting means sewing together layers to make a quilt – usually three layers, so that the finished effect is rather like a fabric club sandwich. The top layer is often patchwork, followed by a padding layer, which is often an old blanket, then the bottom layer, which is often an old sheet.

Quilting is an American pioneer/colonial tradition (though some claim it dates back to the Crusades, and that there is evidence that the ancient Egyptians wore quilted fabrics) with a charming history. Quilting was not only a completely practical way to make quilts for the winter but also an important means of socializing for colonial and pioneer women. This tradition has continued through the decades – the often communal nature of quilting has resulted in some beautiful things being created. The AIDS Memorial Quilt, for instance, was started in San Francisco in 1987, to commemorate people who had died and were not given proper funerals, due to a combination of stigma and many funeral homes' refusal to handle these people's remains. Each friend, lover or family member quilted one part, commemorating one person. At the time of writing, the quilt is still going strong and commemorates 44,000 individuals. It weighs 54 tonnes and is displayed round the world. Some kind souls in America have also created a huge quilt with the names of babies who were born with heart problems – I was contacted about this when my daughter was born in 2004 and she now has her own little square in the quilt, lovingly made for no reason other than kindness by, in our case, complete strangers in the middle of Arkansas. I can actually reduce myself to tears thinking about the beauty and humanity of this, so let's buck up and move on to useful websites:

http://crafts.lovetoknow.com/wiki/Beginner_Quilting
Like it says: a basic how-to.

www.brightcove.tv/search.jsp?query=quilt
Lots and lots of instructional quilting videos.

http://blairpeter.typepad.com/weblog/2007/06/simple_quilt.html
Instructions for making a simple quilt.

www.bean-sprouts.blogspot.com/search/label/crafts
Another simple quilt to make.

www.marirob.blogspot.com/2007/08/baby-gifts-galore.html
Quilted stuff for babies.

www.dsquilts.com
The website of quilting genius Denyse Schmidt, author of *Denyse Schmidt Quilts: 30 Colourful Quilt and Patchwork Projects* (Chronicle, £16.99), which gives step by step instructions and templates for making some truly beautiful quilts and other smaller projects.

All of this crafty goodness leads quite naturally to . . .

Presents

It also doubtless leads to the idea of selling the crafts you produce, once you've refined your skills. We'll get to this on page 116, but first: gifts. One of the things I used to really dislike when I was spending too much money was having to buy someone a present and for that present to be a bit crap – talk about a deeply unsatisfactory double-whammy of expense and mediocrity. I am actually quite good at buying presents, which made it even worse when I couldn't find what I wanted. But you know what it's like: you're in a rush, you're too busy to have afforded the present much thought, your options are limited by time – and you end up by either a) grabbing the nearest vaguely OK thing or b) throwing money at the problem and then feeling really irritated and upset at the amount you've spent – especially if, as is so often the case, the thing you've bought isn't actually very exciting, just tremendously overpriced. So it's not even like it looks amazing, or does anything. It was just expensive, much more expensive than it looks, and it's hardly as though you can tell the present recipient how much you spent. I hate present stress.

Enter crafts. We are, most of us, no matter how interested in tightening our belts, reasonably affluent when it comes to possessions – I mean, you've spent cash on this book, for starters. You're quite rightly interested in saving money, but I think it's fair to assume that you have most of what you need. If you're very young, it may be that there are things you do genuinely need and haven't yet acquired: good saucepans, potato mashers, bookshelves, baby clothes. If you are older, though, you're probably sorted on the pans and bookshelves front. That means presents are lovely indulgences rather than things you actually need. This is where craft presents are especially brilliant.

The alternatives, if you're a person who has their own home and their own stuff to fill it with, are fairly unimaginative and limited: books (always lovely, admittedly), flowers, chocolates, various pretty but pointless knick-knacks, bottles of wine, scented candles . . . The list runs out fairly quickly, and none of it is remotely original, nice as the individual items may be. They don't give the impression of being especially thoughtful presents either, bought specifically with a certain person in mind. I mean, you could give anyone a scented candle, and they'd be pleased and grateful, but they wouldn't think, 'How marvellously thoughtful and original – tailor-made to my tastes.' They'd just think, 'A candle. Nice.'

So not original, not impressively thoughtful and – not cheap. Not cheap at all. It's amazing how expensive the cheapest-looking piece of tat can be. I used to just buy them anyway, but I've recently taken to picking them up and really examining how they're made, and let me tell you – it's not usually terribly impressive. Sometimes I can hardly believe the cheek of the mark-up.

Cards

I find this particularly striking when it comes to cards, as in hand-made greeting cards, which can cost upwards of a fiver for a bit of folded thickish paper with some stuff on it. Solution: make your own cards. Have a look at www.making-greeting-cards.com or www.allcrafts.net/cards.htm (among others) for instructions, templates and inspirations; there are videos showing you how at www.expertvillage.com/video-series/391_card-making.htm. Personally, I wouldn't necessarily bother bogging myself down with too much information: we all know what kind of card we like. You don't have to be especially arty or creative, by the way – a greetings card can be any way you want it to be; it certainly doesn't have to be hand-drawn, or even symmetrical, or even neat. Supplies – glitter, bits of fabric, mini pompoms, ribbon – are all available online, but chances are you have some of these lying about anyway, so just use what you have (and make a box of bits and bobs for future projects) and design your card according to your supplies. You'll probably need glue and scissors, plus possibly a stapler and a needle and thread. Here are some examples of what you might use:

- **Coloured paper and card**. Pretty origami paper is especially useful – you can get it from Muji.

- **Old cards to cannibalize, postcards, invitations, flyers, bits cut out of magazines**, anything at all with a pretty or interesting pattern on it, or with an interesting font, or an especially pleasing word or name.

- **Scraps of fabric**.

- **Sequins, glitter, beads, ribbons, buttons**.

- **Letraset** (if you're feeling ambitious) and ink stamps (ditto).

If you want to gild the lily and make a beautiful envelope (out of anything you have lying around, such as spare bits of old wallpaper), check out www.make-stuff.com/projects/wallpaper_envelopes. html. Or, obviously, take a piece of rectangular card, decorate and fold it, then staple two sides –voila, an envelope. It needs to contain the card and look nice, but it doesn't have to look trad.

Gifts

Now for some gifts to go with the smart card (not necessarily that smart; lovingly hand-made and entirely personalized is the point). Let's start with the easiest presents of all: food. Here are some ideas. All of them are even nicer if you give them with nicely embellished and decorated (and written) labels – 'The damson jam I made for lovely Jane with my own fair hands, 2008' is nicer than 'Damson jam'.

Home-made jam or marmalade.

Home-made chutney or pickle.

Home-made preserves.

Home-grown plants in pretty pots (paint some), either flowering
plants or edible ones. A friend of mine was disproportionately delighted
the other day when I gave her some nasturtiums in an old watering can
(cost: about £1).

Perishable food works too — if you're going to someone's house for
supper, for example, you could take them some home-made cheese
and a loaf of good bread (which you might also have made yourself);
or a cake; or some home-made truffles (pathetically easy – newborns
could do it); or a little jar of home-made pesto. All of these things
are cheaper than a random bottle of wine and ought to be greeted
rapturously, not just because they're nice in themselves, but
because people have come to really appreciate and love the idea
of home-made presents. As I was saying in the Introduction,
what used to be a bit lumpen-seeming and unglamorous
is now viewed as the precise opposite: charming, chic and
desirable. This is so much the case that the poshest shops
now make a specific point of producing (and charging extra
for) wonky-looking goods that could pass for home-made.

There are present ideas scattered throughout this book, but here are some more. If you give crafty presents, I think it's a nice idea to copy my friend Alison (see page 10) and order some name tapes saying 'Made lovingly by Clarabelle' or whatever, to sew into your things. You can get seventy-two basic ones for £3.75 from www.wovenlabelsuk.com; Cash's will do you really chic ones, in a variety of fonts and colours, for marginally more – www.jjcash.co.uk.

You can knit a simple, chunky, short-ish scarf in an evening.

You can crochet a hat or a corsage in an evening.

You can also rustle up knitted toys fairly speedily (don't add buttons or anything swallowable if for small children – embroider eyes etc. instead), as well as knitted cupcakes, flowers and other charming things. Have a look at http://littlecottonrabbits.typepad.co.uk for inspiration, as well as at the blogs listed on pages 100–101 (above).

You can make a cushion cover in much less than an evening.

Sew a felt purse.

Make a fabric scarf.

Rustle up a simple skirt (yeah, I know – I sound mad. But it's entirely possible, especially if you do an elasticated waist).

Make a book bag or a pen holder.

Decorate a cheap blank book inside and out, and turn it into a beautiful journal.

Paint a tiny canvas (with words, if you can't paint, except that everyone can paint a bit – even stick or Weeble-style people look sweet if they're doing something funny or appropriate to your giftee).

Embellish and decorate cheapo hairgrips and box them up nicely (unless you have huge sausage fingers – it's quite fiddly).

Frame a special photograph (as a student, my ex-husband used to do this with photos of himself in full 1980s fashion student rig). I always stock up on frames at pound shops and Ikea (from 50p) for this eventuality. If the frames are ugly, paint or decorate them. If you're in a hurry, paint with clear-setting PVA glue and dip in glitter. When dry and set, paint another layer of glue on top, or varnish.

For special occasions – anniversaries, weddings, birthdays, celebrations – make a really personalized photo album using your photo software. On a Mac, this looks just fantastically beautiful and professional, plus you can add text. Depending on the number of pages, it costs anywhere upwards of £20 and is always met with squeals of delight – all for less money than a vaguely OK photo album would cost, without prints.

Excellent freebie presents: your time. Offer to babysit for a new mum, to give someone a manicure, a piano lesson, a massage, a tidy-up of their house, to cook them a meal, to walk their dog for a week, to collect their kids from school, to sort out their weeding (note that's weeding, not wedding. Don't offer to sort out anyone's wedding, because you'll end up in a straitjacket), etc., etc.

If they're poor and celebrating something, offer them a dinner party (and make Indian vegetarian food, as per page 35). If they're short of space, offer them a drinks party and make punch out of the bottles you'll ask the guests to bring (thousands of recipes online).

Give home-made beauty products. Again, these have escaped the shackles of their hippie past: the posher lines, especially the organic ones, now try and emulate the home-made feel, and charge a premium for it. Now's the time to explore beauty recipes. There's a nice sugar body scrub at www.recipezaar.com/92027, and a whole load of similar ideas online – try www.mybeautyrecipes.com or www.essortment.com/all/homemadebeaut_rigm.htm, or www.treehuggingfamily.com/tag/homemade-beauty-products. For more ideas, see also pages 187–9.

Have a look at some of the following for inspiration for children's presents:

> * *http://blogs1.marthastewart.com/blueprint/2008/03/jodis-board-boo.html*
> Some lovely board book ideas.

> * *www.makeandtakes.com/recycled-chunky-crayons*
> Make recycled chunky crayons.

> * *http://crafts.kaboose.com/gifts*
> Plenty of gift ideas (love the snow globe).

> * *www.designmom.com/2007/12/making-sibling-gifts-2007.html*
> Gift ideas for kids to make other kids.

And don't forget: hand-me-downs are hip again. It is actively lovely to receive children's clothing that has been used by your friends' kids, especially when it comes to clothes for tiny babies. Yes, you could go and buy a brand spanking new outfit for said tiny baby, knowing that it cost a fortune and will last a couple of months – but you could also raid the attic for your old baby clothes (in good nick, obviously), launder and iron them, wrap them in tissue paper and make a lovely big beribboned parcel out of the whole lot. There is something intensely happy-making about seeing an adorable dress, now outgrown by your own daughter, making a friend's daughter look equally sweet.

If a girlfriend has always admired, say, a bracelet you're tiring of, polish it, wrap it prettily and make it her next birthday present. This doesn't come across as cheap, or stingy, or a bit desperate – it comes across as really lovely. There is nothing nicer than a present with meaning or with a bit of emotional subtext.

Keep a present box, if you don't already – recycle unwanted gifts, but stick a note on said unwanted gift reminding you who it's from, so you don't give it back to them (v. embarrassing), or give it to someone else in their presence (worse).

Making Money Out of Your New-found Love of Crafts

Sure, you can sell to friends, and to friends of friends, and you can hire yourself a market stall (pitches cost a great deal less than you might imagine). But we're all short of time, and some of us are a bit shy of standing there in the cold with our home-made tea cosies displayed for all to see. One word: Etsy. www.etsy.com is another whole online world, whose rise and rise has coincided with the crafts explosion. It's basically like a huge crafts mall, or market, containing tens of thousands of little individual stalls run by people who are selling the stuff they make. And the stuff they make is usually amazing. It's been compared to 'a cross

between eBay and your grandma's basement', but that doesn't quite do it justice. It sells absolutely everything you could possibly imagine: big things and tiny things, handmade clothes, bags, accessories, jewellery, bath goods, magazines and books, candles, wedding-cake figurines, frames, ceramics, crocheted stuff, knitted stuff, hats, art (some of it fantastic), patterns, quilts, toys, vintage stuff — and that is the merest tip of the world's biggest iceberg. You can get lost in there for days, which is why, helpfully, Etsy is set out in a user-friendly and manageable way. You can search for items, or look through your local sellers, or browse by colour, or view special showcased items, or read one of their helpful gift guides. It's utterly marvellous and I can't recommend it highly enough.

So, excellent on the shopping front, Etsy goods tend to be inexpensive, sometimes incredibly so (but always check out postage and packing charges if your seller isn't in the UK). It is my number-one port of call if I want to buy someone an original (as in, often, literally one-of-a-kind), lovely, bargainous present. Plus, obviously, you're not lining the pockets of some giant greedy-guts corporation; you're (gently) lining the pockets of a fashion student in Brooklyn, or a mother of four from Dorset who crafts in her spare time, or an elderly lady whose grandchildren have shown her how to sell her knitted beanies online. And you're showing that you support creativity, originality and small (embryonic – zygotic, sometimes) businesses, run by people who are quite like you. Every item you buy from such a person strikes a blow against mass production. Everything about Etsy rocks.

Fancy your own zygotic business? It couldn't be easier. You need a digital camera, to take appetizing shots of whatever creations of yours you want to sell, and that's it. You do everything else online and it's simplicity itself. First, you sign up to Etsy, which is free. You then give yourself a user name, which is also going to be the name of your shop. So if I fancied calling myself Gertrude Bottlenose, my shop's address would be www.gertrudebottlenose.etsy.com – do think carefully about your name, because it's a faff to change it. That's it – you now have an Etsy shop, which you can beautify with banners, biographies and so on. All you have to do next is create a listing, with the help of your photographs and a bit of descriptive nous. The listing costs twenty cents, and Etsy takes a 3.5 per cent (at time of writing) selling fee. The rest is profit. The whole idea is to sell items handmade or customized by you (or handmade/customized by you and some friends, trading, for instance, as Ms Bottlenose & Friends). You can also sell non-handmade crafting supplies and vintage items (twenty years or older).

If you are any good at making anything at all, I strongly urge you to set yourself up with an Etsy boutique. At worst – if literally not a single soul drops by: unlikely, especially if you email people telling them you're in business – you've wasted half an hour of your time. At best, as some of the craft bloggers who have Etsy shops will tell you, you can start earning serious pocket money – after which, of course, the sky's the limit. Anyway, check it out – www.etsy.com. There are chat rooms and forums on the site if you want further help or advice from fellow sellers.

What Not to Scrimp On

If you're going to knit or crochet, buy good-quality yarn made of natural fibres. It may cost more, but it's easier to work with, it lasts longer, it washes better and it doesn't feel all horrible and synthetic. This is especially important if you're knitting for babies or young children. Equally, if you're going to the bother of making a quilt, don't use cheapo (and highly flammable) synthetic fabrics that won't stand the test of time. Your quilt is never going to achieve heirloom status if everyone gets a little electric shock every time they go near it.

Community

*A*s in how to make the best of where you live. Also as in how to enhance your everyday life. And as in how to feel part of a community, even if you think that's a tall order for an urbanite who's never exchanged more than a perfunctory head-nod with any of their neighbours. And, above all, as in how to make your community work for you. We all live sedentary lives and don't tend to engage overly with our immediate surroundings, unless we have small school-age children and do the chatting at the school gates thing. It seems rather a wasted opportunity: many people, I think, feel like tourists in their own neighbourhoods. I say, don't feel like a tourist – own your 'hood. March around it in a proprietorial fashion, even if it's not very pretty (the hood, not your walking style): vigorous walks always result in unexpected, cheering discoveries, and I think it's important to be really familiar with the geography of where you live, especially if you live in a town. In London, if you don't walk, you can end up feeling like a mole. Walking is fat-busting, one of the best modes of getting from A to B, good for your lungs, stress-busting, will (hopefully) provide you with the sunlight necessary to synthesize vitamin D, and – unlike an unpleasant session on the treadmill – is completely free.* Have a look at www.walkit.com for help on planning your walk: enter your starting position and destination and you can print out a map with directions, find out how long it will take you to walk and how many calories you will burn in the process.

---

* *Handy tip for Londoners: go to www.londonwalks.libsyn.com and download free, guided walks as MP3s to play on your iPod. They're brilliant.*

Marching aside, a good starting point might be to read up about your area (I used to have a neighbour who called her genitalia 'my area' – a woefully underused expression, I feel), especially if you are new to it. But even if you aren't, actually you might learn something. As a self-respecting Londoner, it had never occurred to me to go on one of those naff-seeming tourist bus tours, but then I had to show some visitors the sights and thought sitting on the top deck might be a good idea. It turned out to be a brilliant one: I learned lots of new things and had a great time (this often seems to be the way with naff-seeming things: they almost always turn out to be fantastically good fun – see also bingo, Butlins, karaoke and – oh joy – static caravans, pages 217–18). In the same way, exploring the ins and outs of your neighbourhood might throw up a few unexpected gems. I lived in east London for years, for instance, without being aware that the gruesome-looking pub a few streets away did the most amazing Sunday lunches.

People are like sheep and tend to congregate around obvious places, while the more interesting spots quietly get on with it. If you want to know where they are, sites such as www.myvillage.com can be a good starting point;

* I urge you to go to Paris as often as you can; it makes the perfect mini-break. It's gigantically cheaper than going to Manchester, or indeed practically anywhere in Britain – I shall spare you my rant about train fares, but let's just say I've flown to New York for less than it costs to go up north. If you organize yourself well in advance, you can get a return Eurostar ticket from £59 and have a day of pure bliss, eating delicious food and looking at beautiful things for not very much money at all. If you want to stay overnight, Paris, unlike Britain, has the advantage of heaving with clean, cheap, well-located hotels. This isn't the time or the place, but www.tripadvisor.com will point you in their directions; www.cntraveller.co.uk also has an excellent hotels section. See also www.patriciawells.com/paris/photels.htm and the 'charming budget hotels' section of www.parismarais.com. And don't take cabs or public transport – use the Vélibs, or free bicycles, which are available everywhere. I regularly do day trips to Paris and I can't think of anything better designed to really dramatically lift the spirits. Even St Pancras station is beautiful.

I prefer the content-generated ones such as www.trustedplaces.com ('Share what you know, discover what you don't'), a terrific (global) site that often throws up brilliant recommendations for anything from a nice pub to have lunch in to an especially great yoga class or obscure museum. You can customize the site by telling it where you live, though it does cities better than smaller towns. For London (and, handily, Paris*), the excellent www.urbanpath.com is hard to beat. Not only will it give you recommendations for, say, a local hairdresser, but it'll also tell you which stylist to go to if you have curly hair, where to avoid and where to nip into for a cup of tea on the way home. Reviews are written by punters who tell it straight.

Now, obviously, it would be naïve to start from the point of view that we all live in some kind of nirvana and that all of our neighbours are simply heavenly. They do have one advantage, though, which is that they are there, come rain or shine. Get to know them, whether this is over something nice, like a spontaneous neighbourly gathering for drinks, or over something anxiety-causing, like concerns about security: remember, 1) there's safety in numbers; 2) knowledge is power, and knowledge includes familiarity. Say hello to them in the morning, even if they don't say hello back (there is one particular person where I live whom I have greeted cheerfully every day for five years and still not had even a nod in response. It's like a joke. I persevere).

The whole basis of things like Neighbourhood Watch was looking out for each other and each other's property – but you don't need to organize yourself into a time-consuming and slightly curtain-twitching group to achieve the same effect. Knowing your neighbours means being able to go away for the weekend without worrying about who's going to feed the cat, or water your lovingly nurtured lettuces, or keep an eye on your car.

Speaking of cars . . .

City Car Clubs

Car clubs are a pay-as-you-drive alternative to owning a car. It gives all the benefits of clean, modern and reliable cars without the hassle and hidden costs of car ownership.

The following three companies are operating nationwide. Some do yearly memberships and some have a one-off joining fee. The charges vary depending on whether you opt for pay-as-you-go or value packages (a better option if you are going to be using the facility frequently).

* www.citycarclub.co.uk

Bath, Birmingham, Brighton, Bristol, Edinburgh, London, Norwich, Portsmouth

* www.streetcar.co.uk

Brighton, Cambridge, Guildford, London, Southampton

* www.whizzgo.co.uk

Belfast, Birmingham, Brighton, Leeds, Liverpool, London, Manchester, Newcastle, St Albans, Sheffield, Southampton, Winchester, Worcester, York

If there are small children in your street or immediate neighbourhood, make friends with their parents, not only because it's nice, but also because you can then organize:

Free babysitting circles, where you repay your sitter by sitting for her.

Toy-swapping groups, which put an end to piles of garish plastic gathering dust.

The shared purchase and ownership of expensive, big, cumbersome toys, such as those Cozy Coupés toddlers are so fond of. No one has the room to have one as a permanent fixture, but a travelling Cozy Coupé – or huge reinforced paddling pool, or whatever – is a different proposition altogether: much more manageable if you only store it for one or two nights a week and then pass it on. This also has the considerable advantage of maintaining toy excitement, as opposed to toy fatigue.

Trips to the playground, where you take it in turns to take four children for a couple hours, giving three other mothers some peace.

School runs, either by car or on foot – again, it is senseless for four cars/pairs of legs to go and pick up four individual children in the pouring rain, when one person can easily do it and give the others a break. See also www.school-run.org to find other local parents to share the run with.

All of the above are the tip of the iceberg and can be extended in any direction: clothes swaps (see pages 77–8 for the adult version, but think also about children's swaps), cooking double quantities of a favourite recipe one night a week and taking it round to your special nice neighbour, who then repays the favour, giving you both one night off from making supper, etc.

Some less child-specific ideas:

🌸 **Skills-sharing**: rather a horrid expression to describe something really nice, free and very useful. Say I can touch-type, but I can't make jam. I want to know how to make jam – I want to be shown – and I'm happy to repay the favour by typing up a bunch of letters/documents. If I know my neighbours well, I can scoot round to Mrs Bloggs at number 23, famed throughout the borough for her apricot conserve, and offer to do a swap. Better still, if I've been organized about it, I can make myself and my neighbours a little list of our skills. X can garden but Y can do basic electrics, Z can speak French but A can unclog a drain, B can cook but C can teach the piano, D knows how to fish and E has children who'll wash cars, etc., etc. This also applies to intangible skills, like knowledge: if F is a retired schoolteacher who gets knackered walking her dog twice a day and G has kids sitting GCSEs, there's an obvious swap to be made.

🌸 **Shared purchases of large, expensive items, such as lawnmowers**. Unless your garden is a park, you don't need to mow the lawn every day. Buy a really good mower collectively and share it round – that way you only have to store it the odd night, instead of it taking up a large amount of precious space for all eternity (but agree on who's storing it out of season).

🌸 **Shared purchases of smaller, expensive items, or big things that are hard to store, or things that you only use once in a blue moon**. A friend of mine has a travelling preserving pan, for instance, which comes out and does the rounds of her street during the jam-making season.

 Converting physical advantages into financial ones. If someone has large amounts of space, for example, they may like the idea of you all collectively buying a huge chest freezer and sharing the space within it. If they have a huge garden but can't afford a trampoline, they might like the idea of a shared trampoline, available to all of its owners for an hour or so after school.

 Swap stuff: the person whose kids have outgrown their bikes may give them to you in exchange for something you also no longer have the need for.

Share produce: if you grow lettuces and your neighbour grows courgettes, spread the goodness. If your neighbour bakes and you make your own jam, ditto.

Share newspapers, especially on Sundays.

Remember clubs. Book clubs are great, but they're only a starting point: try also cooking clubs, wine clubs, childcare clubs, dog-walking clubs, let's-go-for-a-brisk-walk clubs (if you walk for weight-watching purposes, these are great), holiday clubs that allow you to share each other's second homes, should you be lucky enough to have them, music clubs, singing clubs, let's-go-down-the-disco clubs – the list is endless. Your local borough and county website is the best place to find information about what's available locally, but if the thing you're after doesn't exist, create it yourself. Here are some helpful sites to check out:

* *www.groupomatic.com* gives your group a web page and advice for starting a group or club, attracting members and scheduling events.

* *www.letsgetcooking.org.uk* is a cooking club network.

* *www.ukhandknitting.com* has knitting groups all over the UK.

* check out *www.whyorganic.org/involved_joinAGroup.asp* if you want to get involved with local organic food events, festivals, shared meals and local educational events.

* *www.completerunning.com* has information about how to start your own running club.

And don't forget singing: you don't have to be Maria Callas to join your local choir and it's usually an exhilarating experience.

Recycling

As I was saying at the start of this book, recycling everyday waste has become second nature for most of us. We've seen how to recycle clothes, food and gifts, but you can recycle anything at all, from unwanted ancient computers (which you can't imagine anyone in their right mind being interested in) to the stash of old make-up you've outgrown or grown tired of – and I don't mean getting rid of this stuff by paying someone to come and take it away, which would rather defeat the point.

Freecycle

Freecycle is the most brilliant invention. What it basically is is a huge (just under 5.5 million members at the time of writing), global, online community of people whose mission statement is 'to build a worldwide gifting movement that reduces waste, saves precious resources & eases the burden on our landfills while enabling our members to benefit from the strength of a larger community'. Which is not only laudable, but works absolutely brilliantly.

Simply go to www.uk.freecycle.org and type in your location. You then get directed to your local group, join it (free) and start either posting your unwanted items or snapping up other people's, or both. So, for instance, you'd say 'OFFER: Oxford, Jericho: leaking fridge-freezer, wonky door, white, seen better days, very heavy, needs collecting by Thursday'. Interested parties then email you (it's worth setting up a separate email address, such as a Yahoo one, to deal with this, to save your normal inbox getting flooded). You pick the one you like the sound of most – or the nearest one, or the most efficient or neediest-sounding one – and voila: one leaky fridge with a wonky door gone to a loving home. You then post another message saying the fridge has gone.

It's extremely simple and very effective, and in two years of using Freecycle, I've never had anyone who's been anything other than lovely coming to the door to collect their things (I was worried about nutters, but nutters came there none). Not only does your unwanted item find a good home, but more often than not you are helping people in a very heart-warming way: my daughter's old rocking crib, for instance, was collected by a tired-looking, heavily pregnant young woman who seemed inordinately grateful for it. So you get rid of your unwanted stuff and feel great about it and really help somebody else. It's absolutely brilliant. What is also brilliant is that the undesirability of the item, as perceived by you, has nothing to do with its desirability as perceived by other people. As well as nice, surplus to requirement items like rocking cribs, I've also given away two broken fridges; antique computers (but always run a program that wipes out personal information first); a dead blender with bits missing; a hideous loo seat – it's a long list of duff stuff, which nevertheless had dozens of enthusiastic potential takers.

Needless to say, Freecycle is also a treasure trove if you want stuff, all of it free. A friend recently got a nice, big, fully functioning television from someone much richer who was upgrading to a flat-screen telly; others have obtained sofas, tables, a desk, two computers – you get the idea.

Still on the subject of recycling, most councils are fairly up to speed with all of this. Contact yours for more local information, including how to get a home composting kit or (yow) wormery (and see pages 232–3).

Other Recycling Sites

www.craigslist.org and www.gumtree.com will both let you place free online ads for anything you might want to sell, buy or give away, or anyone you might want to employ. I feel there is nutter potential with these two – lots of perfectly nice-sounding people, but a few clear loonies. Perhaps my judgement has been clouded by the discovery that some people (quite a lot of them) use the former as a handy way of having random sexual encounters in their lunch hour. I feel this sits oddly with looking for an au pair or trying to sell a kitchen table, but don't mind me and my concerns about playing sex Russian roulette (though I do have them. I mean, what's wrong with just picking people up? At least you know what they look like, and you can tell if they're breathing through their mouth, like a rapist). People I know who use Craig's List and Gumtree for domestic purposes assure me that they're both wonderful, non-nut-job resources.

Buying and Selling Locally

I would also strongly encourage you to buy and sell locally, via car boot sales, jumble sales, garage sales, church fairs and the like, and to have a good old clear-out once a year (if you're anything like me and prone to accumulating piles and piles of weird, random stuff). If you're not finding a sale you like the sound of, have your own: all you need to do is post, or stick up, some home-made leaflets. There's a brilliant national car boot sales directory, www.carbootjunction.com, but here's a list of some of the best car boot sales I've found:

Car Boot Sales

In London:

Battersea

Where: Battersea Technology College, Battersea Park Road, London SW11

When: Every Sunday from 1.30 p.m.

Holloway

Where: Opposite the Odeon Cinema, Holloway Road, London N7

When: Every Saturday from 8 a.m. and every Sunday from 10 a.m.

Kilburn

Where: St Augustine's Primary School, Kilburn Park Road, London NW6

When: Every Saturday from 8 a.m.

Outside London:

Brighton, East Sussex

Where: Brighton Railway Station, Brighton

When: Every Sunday from 7 a.m.

Cuffley, Enfield

Where: Junction of Cattlegate Road and Northaw Road, Cuffley

When: Every Sunday from April to September from 7 a.m.

Epsom, Surrey

Where: Hook Road Arena, junction of Hook Road and
Chessington Road, Epsom

When: Every bank holiday Monday from 7.30 a.m.

Hatfield, Hertfordshire

Where: Birchwood Leisure Centre, Longmead, Hatfield

When: Every Sunday from April to October from noon

Leeds, Yorkshire

Where: Harrogate Road/Otley Road, Leeds LS29

When: Every Sunday from 6am

North Weald, Essex

Where: Bluemans Field, on A414 to North Weald,
near Talbot Roundabout

When: Every Saturday from 10.30 a.m.

Orpington, Kent

Where: Hewitts Farm, Court Road, Orpington

When: Every Sunday from 9 a.m.

Books and Libraries

Books make excellent swapping materials, by the way – they are one of the easiest and most popular things to recycle. If you can't or don't do this in person with friends or neighbours, or if your friends or neighbours are freaks who don't read, move house – no, just joking (kind of). Have a look at www.readitswapit.co.uk, which is completely free and like a huge online swap-library. You sign up, make a list of the books you're offering, have a look at 'The Library', which contains tens of thousands of books other people are offering, find a book you want, email its current owner, ask them to have a look at your list to find something they like, and swap.

But don't forget normal libraries either. I feel very passionately about libraries, and very passionately outraged when councils try and close them down. USE YOUR LIBRARY.* It's free, it's warm, it's calming, it's cosy and it contains within it information on every conceivable subject you might be interested in. In case you haven't found yours yet, www.dspace.dial. pipex.com/town/square/ac940/weblibs.html lists every single public library in the UK. And remember, you can not only borrow books for free

---

This section of the book is written from Chalk Farm Library, Sharpleshall Street, London NW1, and one of my favourite places to hang out peacefully. If only it were open five days a week, I'd practically move in.

but, depending on your library's particular set-up, rent cheap DVDs and CDs, games and software, access online encyclopedias, such as *Britannica*, which you would normally have to pay to join, get free wi-fi, have access to cheap printing and photocopying (5p a sheet in my library, 35p at  the newsagent's), find book groups for adults, children, teenagers and families, find homework-help clubs and storytime for toddlers and pre-schoolers, find a local neighbourhood information service, learn about local history, read the papers, use a computer and – sometimes – even have a cup of tea, if there's a café attached. We are blessed – blessed, I tell you – to have free libraries, and most of us don't make nearly enough use of them. Little tip: if your children find it hard to do their homework amidst the chaotic bustle of ordinary family life, pack them off to the library. Concentrates the mind wonderfully, plus they won't have the 'I didn't have the right books' excuse. Libraries are also particularly good for trying out large numbers of children's picture books. Take fifteen out, read them, take them back three weeks later. If your child mourns the loss of *The Little Sausage That Could* (or whatever), buy that title secure in the knowledge that it will be really loved and is likely to remain a favourite.

Women's Institute

Now on to my new obsession, the Women's Institute, and I mean this in a completely non-ironic way. Like everybody else, I used to have a slightly jam-and-Jerusalem view of the WI (not that there's anything wrong with j&J, *au contraire*), and admired it from afar while thinking it wouldn't really have anything to offer me for a good couple of decades, or until I moved to the country. By the time you read this, if everything goes according to plan, I will have set up my own branch of the WI, my own corner of London having sadly lacked an outpost.

My interest was pricked when a rather cool girl-about-town friend and I were trying to make a date to meet. Can't do Tuesday, she said – WI. Can't do Thursday – meeting with X from the WI. Could possibly do the following Monday, but I do so want to go to this talk we're having at the WI. The first time she said 'WI', I assumed she was joking, much as I would have if she'd said, 'Meals on Wheels are coming round to bring me my tea.' 'Why do you keep saying WI?' I eventually asked. 'Does it stand for something other than Women's Institute, like Winsome Iguanas or Wild Intercourse?'

Nope: it stood for Women's Institute. 'It's the coolest thing ever,' my friend said. 'The coolest women, the coolest events, and you should see what speakers we've got lined up – you'd die.' It turned out her local branch was a hotbed of hip, successful women from their thirties up who organized everything from – natch – jam-making sessions to talks by household names to crafting lessons, clothes swaps – and an awful lot of A-list London networking. My jaded, cynical friend has never had so much fun, for so little money, so close to her home. She wasn't the only one: this particular branch became so popular that they had to close membership.

Which set me thinking and made me hotly desirous of joining my local WI. I went to the website – www.thewi.co.uk – and read up on it all. It was founded in 1915, it wants to help you expand your horizons, 'to learn, develop and pass on new skills', it offers 'all kinds of opportunities to all kinds of women', the average age of members in the South is between forty and forty-five and it costs £27 a year to join your local group. Except, I didn't have a local group.

I called up the Women's Institute to find out how one might go about setting up a local branch where one does not exist. It couldn't be simpler. This is what you do:

 Find a handful of like-minded women – the WI recommends ten or so to start with.

 Find a venue.

Contact your local WI adviser (through the website) and she'll talk you through the process, giving you tips and advice.

Invite other women to join, but keep it smallish – the whole point is that you get to know everyone, and part of the point is to get an interesting mix, so don't just invite twenty thirty-year-olds to join.

That's it.

The marvellous thing is that every WI is different, and reflects the interests of its members and community. If you want your WI to have a strong craft bias, or a strong campaigning bias (which it kind of does anyway), or a strong pub bias, it can. If you want to make jam and nothing but jam, you can. You can do whatever you like, provided you are supporting each other and your community, having fun and learning new things. It's marvellous. And all for £27 a year! I honestly think every woman in the country should join.

What Not to Scrimp On

It makes sense, if you are sharing out the cost of expensive items, to buy the best-quality goods you can afford. If, say, a preserving pan is going to travel up and down your street over the years, you want something that will stand the test of time, not some cheapo number that will crack and buckle. And if you're walking, invest in proper walking shoes. You're not going to do yourself any favours marching along in flip-flops.

*T*here are ideas for having fun scattered throughout this book; there isn't a page without a suggestion on it. It kind of depends on what your idea of fun is: some might find making things is fun, or selling things, or giving themselves free wardrobe makeovers, and some might prefer sitting in the pub (in which case, you don't need instructions). What this chapter is concerned with is cheap or free entertainment, from visiting museums to throwing a party.

But I'm actually going to kick off with some of the 'fun' things that are traditionally just expensive and stressful.

Weddings

The first is weddings. The average wedding in the UK costs just under £20,000, which I find simply incredible. To add insult to injury, it's not even like they *feel* expensive: they're often much of a muchness, and it seldom seems as if the bride and groom are having the most special day of their lives.

I say, stop the madness. Weddings are stressful enough in the first place without everyone bankrupting themselves left, right and centre. There is also a direct corollary between expenditure and expectation, and nowhere is this thrown into sharper relief than at a wedding. The more you spend, the more fabulous you (and your guests) expect things to be. Unfortunately, as we've all observed, it doesn't quite work like that. Massively expensive weddings are often the ones where the bride sits at the top table with a slightly disgruntled look on her face because she knows exactly how much each glass of fizz, each canapé and each flower has cost — it's cost the earth — and she doesn't feel she's getting her quid's worth. This is not what a person should be doing on their wedding day. It doesn't really add to the general gaiety of the occasion. It can even ruin it.

JUST MAR

Hen and Stag Parties – a Plea

Quick detour . . . I've observed, over the past few years, that people's hen and stag parties are getting more and more elaborate, and more and more expensive. It's gone beyond a joke: it is now not that unusual to be expected to take a week off work, book flights and accommodation, find some spending money and an appropriate wardrobe, and go hotfooting it to somewhere nobody can really afford to go to, either time- or money-wise, there to joyously celebrate the forthcoming nuptials.

Um . . . can I just say? Your friends are glad for you, but they're not that glad.

Here's the deal: it is completely socially unacceptable behaviour for the bride- or groom-to-be to make this kind of demand. It's too big an ask. The whole thing is really embarrassing and awkward for your poor friends, who want to celebrate with you and so do somehow find the time off/money/childcare, but who secretly resent you for having forced them into it. Despite what they might be saying to your face, they've probably had a good moan behind your back.

I can't say I blame them. Asking people to go on these protracted hen/stag events is the most tiresome imposition. There is only one circumstance where it is permissible (sorry to sound like an etiquette guide, but I think a little etiquette lesson is required). This is if you can afford, either through circumstance or through giant saving up, to pay for each and every one of your guests. You want to take ten girlfriends on a spa holiday at your own expense? Go right ahead. Can't afford it? Too bad – I'm afraid it's the pub and the comedy breasts and L-plates for you.*At least it is if you're completely unimaginative.

---

*Unless your kind friends offer to take you to a spa or a hotel or wherever. Offering is good. Bossing people into doing something they don't really want to do is bad, bad, bad.

With a little forethought, though, it is perfectly possible to organize a fun evening out without breaking the bank. The clue is in the word 'evening', which isn't the same as 'weekend' or 'week'.

At the very least, please always consult with your hen/stag party first, rather than presenting them with a fait accompli. Not everyone likes spas, or white-water rafting, or hiring a massive country mansion for the weekend and lolling about pretending to be debutantes (quite a weird one, that, and increasingly popular), and if you're expecting people to pay for the privilege, it is basic good manners to run the idea past them first.

This, incidentally – the difficulty of finding one thing that everyone likes doing – is why the traditional take on hen/stag parties came into being. Not to put too fine a point on it, everyone likes having a drink and most people can afford an evening of this kind. I say, if it ain't broke, don't fix it. And if you're too old to run around getting legless all over town, have a nice dinner instead.

This plea, incidentally, applies to all OTT celebrations in general. It is not cool to invite people to your thirtieth, or fortieth, or fiftieth, and expect them – surprise! – to pay for the privilege because you're so incredibly special. You friends are pleased it's your birthday but, again, not that pleased. You want to hire a restaurant? You pay. You want a cocktail party? You buy the drinks. The weird idea that everyone is so happy for you that they're really delighted to spend £50 a head on a dinner they didn't really want, plus a cab home, plus a babysitter, is completely out there – I don't understand where it's come from, but I think it's high time people knocked it on the head. It's one away from asking people to a kitchen supper and charging them for it. If you hanker after some kind of extravaganza, have one – but save up for it, and pick up the bill yourself.

Now I've got that off my chest – it's been bothering me for years – on to weddings. Oh no – one last thing. If you're getting married, for God's sake please don't ask for cash as a present. This is another growing trend and it is GHASTLY – greedy, shameless and beyond vulgar. It takes all the pleasure out of getting a wedding invite.

As I was saying, £20,000 on average. Look, I do understand: it's your big day and you want it to be wonderful and memorable, and you think that means extravagant expense. I can only (obviously) write subjectively, but I have been to a gigantic number of weddings of all kinds over the years and these are my observations:

The two best – as in most beautiful and most memorable – wedding dresses in recent memory were a) vintage from eBay and b) made by a friend of the bride's. The meringues, even the ones that cost thousands upon thousands, all melt away into one big meringue-shaped blur and I have no recollection of any of them. Ask yourself, before coughing up thousands on that big designer number: do you want your guests to remember what you wore? Because if so, you might want to try something a little bit more original than metres of hugely expensive pouffy white stuff.

The four best parties were a) and b) in the local community hall, c) in an empty warehouse space that had been 'dressed' for the occasion and d) in someone's parents' garden. Unless you are socially anxious enough to want to create a false impression – the pretence that you are in fact a princess, or the pretence that your family is always hanging out at deluxe country hotels – remember that all you need is a space that works. The space can be bare. The space can be familiar. The space can be down the road. It can be wedged between a kebab shop and a home for tramps. Nobody cares – they're going to be inside having a great time. If it's an old church hall and you went to ballet lessons in it as a child, so much the better – it will have emotional resonance as well as seating the right number of guests. Any space can be transformed: don't shun the obvious (and cheap) just because it's plain. Plain is good: you can dress it up exactly how you want, and dressing a space isn't expensive – what costs is room hire.

The best meals were a) huge shared plates of robust home-style food and b) curry. There is very little point in having expensive 'posh' wedding food, because it is seldom the thing people want to eat. Remember that people are always starving by the time they sit down at weddings. They've sat through the ceremony, made their way to the next venue, had drinks, milled about, made small talk to complete strangers, queued for the loo. What they want is a large drink and a plate of good food to soak it up with, not some namby thimble of champagne and a bit of poached salmon.

The best wine was free-flowing and cheap. As above, there isn't much point in spending money on exquisite wine, because, frankly, nobody will notice. Weddings are very drinky occasions, not least because you need Dutch courage, as a guest, to see you through the day – all that chatting to strangers is thirsty work. The point is quantity rather than quality, though obviously I'd steer clear of actual gut-rot (actually, when I was seventeen or so I went to a friend's wedding where they served Thunderbird and hash wedding cake. I don't remember much about it, but it now strikes me as rather chic. And sweetly old-fashioned – the current supermodel option would be crack and vodka).

I can't tell the difference between professionally hired DJs and ones that are friends of the married couple, or friends of friends, and I don't think it's because I am particularly cloth-eared. If someone offers to do the music for you as a favour (or as a wedding gift), give them a little try-out and then say yes. Wedding bands/discos cost a fortune. Spend your money on the best sound system you can afford instead – at which point, even a well-uploaded iPod would do, frankly. People want to dance, not to watch some plonker throwing hand shapes and being down with va kidz.

The stiffer the wedding, the more boring and samey-feeling for the guests. Weddings are a prime example of people at their most sheep-like, thinking they're following 'tradition'. Actually, there are no traditions when it comes to receptions. The tradition is in the exchange of vows; nowhere is it inscribed that you have to spend money hand over fist. You can have any kind of celebration you like. If you want to have a wedding picnic on a beach, do it. If you don't want everyone to dress like a penguin/waiter, ask them not to. It's your day: reclaim it from the tyranny of bridal magazines!

Speeches and readings are hugely important. If someone's not a good public speaker, don't get them to make a speech – it's just embarrassing. If people are rubbish at reading, don't get them to read. Harsh, but necessary. Bad speeches can ruin about an hour's worth of wedding party – and that hour goes by v-e-r-y slowly for everybody.

Weddings that are complete fantasy – as in weddings that bear no recognizable relation to anything at all about the married couple – are sometimes just plain weird. This includes weddings in random hotels, which often feel slightly like old people's homes, with their unappetizing cooking smells and ugly carpets. The best wedding receptions are either in someone's home, or in someone's garden, or in a 'blank' space that has been decorated for the occasion.

The grander the wedding, the higher the expectation, the more likely you are to feel disappointed, either as a participant or as a guest.

The more relaxed-feeling the wedding, the more well disposed and chilled your guests are going to be.

Snobby thing to say, but posh weddings don't feel posh (unless they're really posh). There's always some scruffy-seeming, home-made element: wild flowers jumbled together in jugs, or random dogs wearing diamanté necklaces, or the bride resplendent in granny's wedding dress. Unposh weddings – all formal and stiff and 'by the book' – try to replicate something that doesn't actually really exist anywhere outside of stately homes with their own private chapels. They're doomed to failure: the benchmark is too high, and besides, why ape something faintly absurd? This echoes my point in the Introduction: perfection, or rather the striving for an imaginary perfection, has become a bit naff. If you want a truly smart wedding, the first thing to do is to relax.

People who arrive on horseback, or in a carriage, look like they never got over Cinderella. Sweet if you're twenty, less so if you're thirty-eight.

There is something comical about real grown-ups – thirty- or forty-something women, especially ones with children – doing the whole 'virgin bride' thing in pristine white silk. It doesn't really wash and, again, you run the risk of looking delusional, or just plain bonkers – unless you are of course virgo intacta. I personally think absolutely no white meringues over the age of thirty, especially if you're getting married in church: save money and your dignity. (I am admittedly overly superstitious, but starting married life pretending to be something you're not – a pure and innocent virgin – before the eyes of God seems pretty strange to me, like an adult woman taking her First Communion in a little white dress and plaits and long white socks. You'd slightly want to knock on her head and shout, 'Hello?')

What all of the above are trying to prove is that how good a wedding is bears no relation to how much it has cost. I'm not making these observations because they happen to be convenient (although they are), but because they're genuine. Having a cheap wedding is a very real possibility – it'll still be wonderful, and the only person aware of the cost-cutting will be the person paying. The number-one port of call for more ideas than you'll know what to do with is www.moneysavingexpert.com/health/cheaper-weddings, followed by www.cheap-wedding-success.co.uk, both of which are absolutely packed with ideas, advice and tips from happy (and not broke) brides. There is more information online than I can give you in this book, but here, nevertheless, are some basic ideas of mine, followed by some additional websites you may find useful.

The Dress

Think outside the meringue, as above. What you want is a beautiful dress that makes you feel absolutely amazing. There is no rule that says that dress exists only in a bridal shop. If you're overwhelmed trying to track it down, use a personal shopper. The larger department stores, such as Selfridges in London, offer this service free of charge; smart local boutiques can also advise you informally if you share your quandary. Talk to people and always ask for help: if you can't see what you want, it doesn't mean the buyer can't procure it. Also use eBay, and ask your friendly vintage shop owner to look up some frocks that might make good wedding dresses, but ask well in advance, obviously, and try not to be too vague about the type of thing you're after (unless you really trust the shop owner's taste). Note 1: good underwear is crucial – don't scrimp. Note 2: personal stylists are very expensive, but if you're busy and stressed and they can find your dream wedding dress under budget and in one afternoon, the cost may be worth it. I really rate Anne Hamlyn of Dress Me, www.dressme.biz. And note 3: you can hire wedding dresses – there's a list of rental places at www.freeindex.co.uk/categories/shopping/clothes/Wedding_Dress_Hire.

Make-Up

Everyone knows someone who's brilliant at make-up. Ask that person to do yours – or learn to do your own (see page 193). I know people who hired super-expensive make-up artists for their big day and were disappointed by the results – and, worse, were too embarrassed to say. A friend knows your face and your style, plus they're your friend, so you can have practice runs, and be explicit about your likes and dislikes without feeling in thrall, or that you have to be polite. This is quite a big favour to ask of someone, so request it as a wedding present. If all your friends are cack-handed (unlikely), go and eye up the people who work at make-up counters in your local department store. Some will be trained make-up artists (e.g. everyone who works on MAC counters), and may agree to do your make-up for a fraction of the cost of a bridal specialist.

Hair

If you can't do your own hair, try friends or friends of friends – again, most of us know someone who's handy with a brush. Other tip: try the old-fashioned salon that does OAP specials. They're usually brilliant at putting hair up in an old-school glam style. Note that old-fashioned salons – the ones with rows of hoods and stylists called Mr Tony – are generally an excellent and ultra-bargainous bet for any kind of serious, 'done' party hair, especially if you like that shampoo-and-set Dita Von Teese look.

Flowers

Fresh, wild-looking flowers are far chicer and more fashionable than stiff arrangements. If you're a rural sort, pick your own (and don't stop at flowers – wheat is beautiful, as is blossom, as are berries, as are twigs). If you're a townie, either make a trip to the countryside or go to your nearest flower market early in the morning (do a dry run a couple of weeks before) and stock up on armfuls of cheap blooms. If you really want something fairly formal, go and ask for help in your local church (as in asking ladies who do flowers to help you, not as in asking for direct intervention from the good Lord, though I suppose the latter is always worth a pop).

The Car

If you know anyone at all – a friend, a neighbour, your auntie's mate Darren's brother's ex-wife – with a glamorous car, ask them, as charmingly as possible, whether it would be possible to borrow it. It's quite hard to turn down a polite, friendly request for the loan of your car if that loan means making a huge difference to someone's wedding day. A friend of mine even left a message on the windscreen of a car she liked that was parked locally – it was a little illustrated poem, actually, and had her phone number on it. The man called her back and lent them his car. Another friend has (twice) emailed people she found selling their cars online and bagged herself a free Roller for the day (and a driver – the seller insisted on driving for insurance reasons). Bloke's selling his car, car's just sitting there: he may well have a poetic soul and lend it to you for nothing, or rent it to you for cheap. Don't just ask bluntly, though – you stand more chance of success if you're charming and/or funny.

Photographs

Obviously you want proper pictures. But it's a lot easier to get proper pictures now we all have digital cameras. It used to be that professional photographers were the only option, because no one could see what the pictures looked like until they were printed, and no one wanted to run the risk of everything being wonky or out of focus. That's all changed: with a digital camera, you can see instantly whether the picture is good or bad. Unless you are after very formal portraits, I'd rely on friends and family, each armed with their own camera, to chronicle your day in images. You can check what they've done at any stage and get them to take more if you don't like the existing ones. It's also a good idea to ask anyone who has one to bring their camera and take shots throughout the reception – a modern update on having disposable cameras at the table. It doesn't cost anyone anything, the prints can be emailed free and you end up with a brilliant selection to chose from and have printed.

The Cake

Wedding cake: the cost of the cake is in the finish, not in the ingredients, but I feel the stress of making your own is likely to be overwhelming, unless you are an accomplished cake-maker. This doesn't apply if you like cupcakes, though. Several weddings I've been to recently had beautiful tiered cupcake towers, with each cupcake individually iced. They looked amazing and tasted delicious, and anyone can make cupcakes (they're stupidly expensive to buy). Here is the ultimate vanilla cupcake recipe, from the Magnolia Bakery in New York.*

* Source: © Allysa Torey, More from Magnolia: Recipes from the World Famous Bakery and Allysa Torey's Home Kitchen, Simon & Schuster, 2004

Cupcakes

Makes about 30

180g self-raising flour
150g plain flour
250g softened unsalted butter
500g caster sugar
4 large eggs
285ml milk
1 teaspoon vanilla essence
Vanilla Buttercream (recipe follows)

1. Preheat the oven to 180°C/350°F/gas mark 4.

2. Line your muffin tins with cupcake papers.

3. In a small bowl, combine the flours and set aside.

4. In a large bowl, on the medium speed of an electric mixer, cream the butter until smooth. Add the sugar gradually and beat until fluffy, about 3 minutes.

5. Add the eggs, one at a time, beating well after each addition.

6. Add the dry ingredients in three parts, alternating with the milk and vanilla. With each addition, beat until the ingredients are incorporated but do not overbeat.

7. Using a rubber spatula, scrape down the batter in the bowl to make sure the ingredients are well blended. Carefully spoon the batter into the cupcake liners, filling them about three-quarters full.

8. Bake for 20–25 minutes, or until a cake skewer inserted in the centre of the cupcake comes out clean.

9. Cool the cupcakes in the tins for 15 minutes. Remove from the tins and cool completely on a wire rack before icing.

Vanilla Buttercream

225g softened unsalted butter

600–800g icing sugar
(this is not a typo! It's just a great big lot of sugar)

125ml milk

2 teaspoons vanilla essence

1. In a large bowl, on the medium speed of an electric mixer, cream the butter until smooth.

2. Add about 500g of the sugar and then the milk and the vanilla. Beat until smooth and creamy, about 3–5 minutes.

3. Gradually add the remaining sugar, a bit at a time, beating well after each addition (about 2 minutes), until the icing is thick enough to be of good spreading consistency. You may not need to add all of the sugar.

4. If desired, add a few drops of food colouring and mix thoroughly. (Use and store the icing at room temperature because it will set if chilled.) Icing can be stored in an airtight container for up to 3 days.

The Honeymoon

❀ **Ask like mad to borrow someone's house** (again, don't just ask rudely – ask for this as a wedding present). Honeymoons are about the bliss of being alone with your brand-new spouse. They're quite often spent horizontally. Yes, it would be nice to spend yours in a palazzo in Venice, but you may find a well-appointed cottage in Suffolk does an equally good job, for free.

🌸 **Do a house swap**. There are many sites, of which the best is www.homeexchange.com (and see pages 222–3). All you need to find is your plane fare and money for food; use of a car is often included. House swaps allow you to go to amazing places that you wouldn't find yourself in in the ordinary course of things. Tip: plan well ahead and communicate honestly with your swapper. Don't big up your house or area — just tell the truth, and give them plenty of detail, to avoid spending your honeymoon explaining the tumble dryer's idiosyncrasies.

🌸 **Think about renting a property yourself**, rather than relying on hotels and special honeymoon packages. You would be amazed at how cheaply you can rent wonderful beach houses in America and Australia; that Venetian palazzo (or an apartment in one) may also come in surprisingly under budget. Giant advantage: the maid doesn't knock on the door every morning shouting, 'I BRING TOWELS!' mid-shag.

🌸 **Last honeymoon tip: if you really have no money, spend it at home**. Unplug the computer, unplug the phone, switch off your mobile, buy whatever treats you can afford, draw the curtains, get lots of candles, make delicious food, and take to bed for the weekend with a supply of condoms (or not, as you see fit — now you're married and all), snacks, alcohol and your favourite films on DVD. A little extra money gets you a visit from a masseuse, a gourmet takeaway and a cleaner to tidy up after you. What's not to love?

Handy Websites

📔 *www.diybride.com*

📔 *www.ethicalweddings.com*

📔 *www.epicurious.com/recipesmenus/holidays/wedding/recipes*

📔 *www.creditpanda.com/blog/2007/50-ways-to-save-money-on-your-wedding*

Christmas

Another time of year when our credit cards take extreme abuse and all our stress levels go stratospheric, and for what? One day. Not even one day, really – about six hours. Now, I am obsessed with Christmas. I love it. I don't quite know why I go such a bundle on it, except that I have well-developed matriarchal tendencies and I like to give them full rein once a year. Also, I want my children to remember their Christmases, so I don't vary anything from year to year; Christmas is the one time when tradition is king. The tree comes on the 15th, we decorate it that evening, their fathers do the lights and the drinks, the children and I do the baubles, and we put the fairy on right at the end, with some ceremony; then, on the 16th, we start cooking. We're usually somewhere between eighteen and twenty-two on Christmas Day itself, and I love every minute of it. But . . . But . . . It had become *unbelievably* expensive in recent years – not just the presents for twenty people, but the wrapping paper, the drinks, the snacks to keep you going until lunch (at about 4 p.m., in our case), the food itself, etc., etc. I was still paying for Christmas in June. You know how you do Christmas, and how you like it, so I don't want to be prescriptive, but this is what I now do to save me time and money:

If there are a large number of you, agree with each other to only give presents to the children.

If that's an unbearable prospect (I feel your pain), agree on a set budget – £5, £10, £20 – per present per head, and make it clear that busting the budget is not an option.

Make everyone bring something, matching your request to their income. Last year I efficiently sent everyone an email making them responsible for one aspect of Christmas Day: flowers, candles, napkins (after years of kitchen roll), snacks to have with drinks, Christmas puddings, brandy butter and so on. One ex-husband did white wine, another red wine; I did champagne (award-winning number from Waitrose*); someone swotted up on cocktails (to eke out the champagne); another person brought their karaoke CDs; the children were responsible for laying the table; my least financially buoyant but most creative friend decorated the sitting room with stuff from our attic, and so on and so forth. This saved money (and how), but it was also unbelievably helpful. Instead of running around like a blue-arsed fly, 'all' I had to do was produce the food. Allocated tasks don't have to involve expense. Get the teenagers on washing-up duty, with one on stand-by for emergency trips to the corner shop; put aunties in charge of Disney DVDs for the toddlers; ask energetic sorts to take the dog for a walk while you load the dishwasher (for the third time), and so on.

Presents

If the present thing is manageable because there aren't piles of you, give family members lists of what you'd like. I know this isn't very romantic, but a) it saves you from being given piles of crap you don't want and b) it means everyone gets presents they actually need or desire. If you don't actually need anything except for a big thing – a new bicycle, for instance – everyone can cobble together the money and give it collectively. If they can't quite stretch that far, ask for something cheaper, or tell them you'd be happy with half a bike to be getting on with.

* *This one, in fact: www.independent.co.uk/life-style/food-and-drink/news/ top-marque-for-supermarket-in-the-champagne-stakes-763575.html.*

Start shopping early, like six months ahead, and try and do as much of it as possible online. Not only does this cut down on stress levels, but it spreads the cost. The nightmare of Christmas has a lot to do with the shocking credit card bills you get in January. If you spread out your expenses over the previous months, you don't get the huge bill, ergo you don't start the New Year feeling sick at how much you've spent.

If you physically have to hit the shops, go shopping on the 23rd, when the shops are quieter. If you have nerves of steel, the 24th is better still. The 21st and 22nd are hopeless – everywhere is packed.

If you've left everything late and feel panicky, head to Argos, which opens early, closes late and has extremely competitive prices, and where it is possible to find pretty much something for everyone. It does involve wading through a certain amount of dross, admittedly, but the choice is massive.

Avoid the obvious places – whatever your local equivalent of Oxford Street is – and shop in smaller, quirkier neighbourhoods. You get cheaper, better, more original presents, and half the crowds.

Make as many presents as possible – see the Crafts and Food chapters. Don't start doing this on 20 December. I try and make little things throughout the year, and keep them in my present drawer. If you're making edible presents, check they don't need refrigerating and won't go off/melt sitting under the tree.

Get the children to make presents too. Nobody doesn't like a giant beribboned box of home-made fudge. More edible present ideas here: www.wondertime.go.com/life-at-home/article/mommys-little-helpers.html. Teenagers often make brilliant music compilation CDs – an excellent gift for the middle-aged kidult.

Start wrapping in early December – just a few every night as you're watching telly. Saves being up till 2 a.m. on Christmas morning and running out of Sellotape.

Assemble anything that needs assembling well in advance. Saves you discovering, at midnight on Christmas Eve, that the manufacturer forgot to include screws or instructions for the self-assembly play house.

Use recycled wrapping paper. I personally also love brown paper with coloured string, and newspaper with beautiful ribbon (from the haberdasher's – enough dazzling ribbon for everybody for a fraction of the price of ordinary wrapping paper). You can use whatever you have to hand: bits of magazine or catalogue, old calendars (nicely seasonal), old posters, old wallcharts, old maps, the horoscope page (pick a good one). Not only do they look nice, but you can tailor the wrapping to the giftee: a magazine picture of a shell-strewn beach for your surfer friend, a free wallchart of common or garden birds for Old Mr Smoothie who's still sowing his oats, and so on.

Recycle last year's Christmas cards by snipping them and turning them into gift tags, and make your own Christmas cards (or send e-cards). See www. kidscraftweekly.com/cards_issue.html for ideas.

Food and Drink

Remember the weird rule about food and numbers, which is, the more people you have, the less food you need. I don't really understand how this works, but it's absolutely true. Every year I go and do my giant Christmas shop with my friend Sophia, and every year she says, 'That's a ridiculous amount of potatoes/sprouts/parsnips/cranberries.' Every year I roll my eyes and say, 'But there are twenty of us!' And every year she is proved right (last year we had too many roast potatoes, a thing I'd have found unimaginable if I hadn't seen it with my own eyes). Trust your butcher re turkey size and trust the size of your plate for the rest. Remember that it is physically impossible to fit giant amounts of turkey, bread sauce, cranberry sauce, roast potatoes, sprouts 'n' pancetta, roast parsnips, stuffings and pigs in blankets on an ordinary-sized dinner plate. Bear this in mind by visualizing the plate when you're shopping (and cooking), and you'll save yourself a packet and not produce much waste.

- **The Soil Association reckons that a typical Christmas dinner can rack up 49,000 miles in imported ingredients**, which is equivalent to two journeys around the world. Christmas is stressful enough without giving yourself a guilty conscience, so take this fact and make of it what you will – but remember that air miles are obviated by buying seasonal and local.

- **Don't scrimp on the turkey**. Just don't. Buy the poshest, most Bronzy, most organic turkey you can. There is no point or pleasure in eating battery death-bird on Christmas Day (or any other day).

- **If you're buying the wine yourself, read up on the inevitable Christmas wine round-ups before you shop**. Remember that some supermarket own-brand champagnes and sparkling wines regularly come out top, or near the top, in blind tastings; the same is true of affordable wine. Most people cannot really tell the difference between a £6 and a £16 bottle anyway, is the truth of it, no matter how expert they may consider themselves. And don't forget mulled wine – an excellent way of making cheap red go a long way. Ensure that you have headache pills in the house for the inevitable hangover.

- **Doing the Christmas food shop online**, with a carefully compiled list, will save you from all those impulse buys and save you many a quid. You don't need a family-sized tin of factory-produced biscuits which is marked up because it has robins on it. Make your own – cheaporama and nicely festive-feeling.

- **Not really food, but baubles tend to be on the expensive side**. If you've smashed a few since last year, or if your tree's got bigger and now has annoying gaps, make hard biscuits, ice them and attach them to the tree with ribbons. There's a recipe of Nigella Lawson's for these at www.bbc.co.uk/food/recipes/database/christmas_84679.shtml.

Parties

Moving swiftly on, I am a great believer in having as many parties as possible – actually, I am a great believer in making your own entertainment full stop. The smoking ban has, for many people, taken some of the fun out of going out, and besides, even an ordinary evening out now costs so much money that it has become prohibitive.* It's also led to a huge rise in swizz syndrome, where you come home with the annoying feeling that your evening cost too much money and wasn't that much fun. Having parties yourself is much easier than relying on other people and costs a fraction of the price of an ordinary night out. I'm not talking about giant parties – though those are nice too – but about all kinds of parties: brunch parties, lunch parties, tea parties, drinks parties, children's parties, karaoke parties, dinner parties, the lot. Here are some general tips:

If you just want to get together with some friends, ask everyone to bring something to eat and make punch. There's something rather *Desperate Housewives* about the idea of people turning up with rice salad in a Tupperware box, but don't knock it. You get an instant meal without having lifted a finger and quench your thirst by spending less money than it costs to buy a round of drinks in a bar. The other thing about getting people to bring stuff is that it immediately makes them a participant, not an observer, which is what you want at parties.

* *Plus, in London at least, Thursday and Friday nights in town involve negotiating packs of aggressive drunks and rivers of sick.*

If you want to go rather more sophisticated, make cocktails. Eight of you could drink yourselves into a stupor for the price of a bottle of vodka and a couple of mixers, which works out at about £2 a head, £3 if you want to go really mad and fall into an alcoholic coma. There are hundreds of cocktail recipes online. Tip: pick one and stick with it – you will feel like death the next day if you mix and match.

See pages 36–7 for cheap dinner party food.

Brunch parties are jolly and brilliantly cheap: newspapers, omelettes or pancakes, Marys Bloody or Virgin, the *EastEnders* omnibus. Perfect Sunday, really.

Tea parties: make a cake, make some scones (takes 10 minutes), make some tea. Serve on/in pretty china. Cost: minimal. Feels very grown-up and is an excellent way of seeing people for a finite amount of time, if it's work rather than pleasure, say – unlike at other parties, people leave when tea is over, plus, in a thrifty double-whammy, you're usually too stuffed to want supper that night.

Karaoke parties: you can hire karaoke machines, but I feel that buying them is a sound investment – mine has given me years of pleasure. It's called the Magic Sing and it's just a mike that you load up with different song chips: i.e. it's tiny and doesn't take up any space (see www.magicsingkaraoke.co.uk). You then plug the mike into your telly and bellow away for hours on end, bringing joy to your neighbours. I am also a great fan of SingStar, especially SingStar 80s, which works on my children's PlayStation 2. Note that karaoke parties need alcohol.

Pampering parties: where you and some girlfriends lounge about giving each other facials and makeovers. Very soothing, especially if *Sex and the City* is on in the background, plus you get to play with other people's make-up. Do not underestimate the pampering party, despite its silly name: everyone likes it, whether they're twelve or sixty-two, and, you know, you're worth it.

Sleepover parties: not just for children. If you have a spare room, or if you can persuade your children to bunk up together for a couple of nights, you can have adults to stay too. Long boozy dinner on Friday night, brunch on Saturday, a bracing walk, a fire and more drinks and a cosy supper, a trip to the movies, perhaps, or an exhibition on Sunday morning – it can be really enjoyable. I used to rent a country house and have vast numbers of people to stay every weekend, and when I had to give it up (couldn't afford it any more, natch), I continued the weekend guest tradition in my London house. You don't need a country cottage to have house parties.

A note on decorating for parties: if you want to be thrifty, keep it simple. I find it's mostly to do with lighting – you don't want too much unflattering brightness. Dim the lights, stick nightlights in jam jars and candles in candlesticks, buy some flowers (you don't have to have very many: individual flowers in individual glasses or jars, or even cans, look beautiful) and you're done.

Children's Parties

Now, these are a different story: impromptu doesn't really work. I could rant for about ten pages on the ridiculousness of some children's parties and the insane amounts of money people spend on them. I'm old-school, I'm afraid — I might stretch to a bouncy castle every now and then, but that's my limit. My children have, over the years, gone to children's parties which featured the following: single orchids hung in individual glass vials from the ceiling; a temporary synagogue which turned into a temporary discotheque; a party for three-year-olds in a palatial minimalist flat,

where each child sat in splendour at an enormous table, with a single silver balloon attached to each chair, and was served Thai fusion food; a fully catered, fully staffed toddlers' party in a marquee; a party where the parents had hired ponies and traps; a party where the cake, creepily, was a life-size replica of the child. Some of these parents were rich, but by no means all of them were — it's just people have become so competitive about kids' parties that they feel obliged to spend insane amounts of money in the process. Do the children enjoy such parties? Not in my experience, no. Small children like running around, getting messy, getting wet and eating cake. Bigger children like dressing up, magic, princesses or football, and eating cake. It's not rocket science and it doesn't have to cost the earth. You don't need an entertainer if you have an ample supply of games up your sleeve, provided you adopt a sergeant-majorish approach to organizing them. (And you can always be the entertainer, though again I'd advise against anything too impromptu: have your schedule worked out.) So I'd like to make a plea for a return to old-fashioned, jelly-and-ice-cream children's parties. These are inexpensive, wildly popular with kids and don't set a crazy precedent in terms of extravagance. Don't get stressed out about party bags either. I have found the most economical way of doing these is to buy one affordable toy or book, rather than an array of cheapo party favours (which seem cheap individually but aren't collectively, and anyway break within ten minutes), and stick it in a (paper, home-decorated) bag with a big slice of cake. That's it. No complaints thus far and it's been fifteen years since I started having children's parties.

Here are some websites that will help and inspire you:

http://party.kaboose.com/index.html
A great American website packed with ideas for themes and cakes (including recipes) for children of all ages.

www.kids-party.com
100 party game ideas.

www.dltk-kids.com/crafts/birthday/index.html
Another American site with banners, hats, cards and game templates to print out.

www.boardmanweb.com/party/party_themes.htm
Select a theme and get lots of ideas for invitations, decorations, food and activities.

www.facepaintingdesigns.co.uk/designs/designs.html
Step-by-step instructions for face painting a number of different designs.

http://familyfun.go.com/recipes/special/specialfeature/cakefinder-birthday
Lots of ideas for birthday cakes to make.

www.supercook.co.uk/inspiration/recipe-ideas/kids-birthday-party
Some great birthday cake recipes.

www.evite.com
Send online invitations – cheaper, greener, easier.

www.partygameideas.com/familypartygames.htm
One for family games, where there are a mixture of adults and children.

Other Ways of Having Fun at Home

Board Games

Now on to less organized, smaller ways of having fun. Number one is board games, which have seen a huge resurgence in recent years, not least due to the popularity of online word games, such as the late, lamented Scrabulous (like Scrabble) and Scramble (like Boggle) on Facebook. Facebook itself – www.facebook.com – along with MySpace and others like it, is a free source of quite a lot of fun. I didn't see the point of it when a friend persuaded me to join, but a year down the line I think the point is partly this: I am 'in touch' with a number of people I like enough to be curious about but don't necessarily want (or have the time) to actually see in the flesh. For me, though, the greater point is that Facebook is a valuable tool in my ongoing Alzheimer's prevention programme, because of its word games. I play these on a daily basis and I do feel, rightly or wrongly, that they both keep me more mentally agile than I would be otherwise. Also, they're really fun.

Anyway, board games. The vast majority of people love these, the exception being people who hate to lose so much that they'd rather not play in the first place. If it's been a while since you explored the joys of Yahtzee, I suggest you start by playing with family members to refresh your skills, then broaden the board games evening concept out to include friends. Remember, it's hard to eat and play at the same time, so either ask people to eat first or serve something easy that everyone can wolf down before concentrating on to the business at hand. Note also that you don't want too many people at a games evening, unless you have double the games – two Scrabble boards and so on. You can, of course, also have another kind of evening altogether, where you have large numbers of people and different games going on in each room, rather in the manner of a dubious 'lady' running a gaming house during the Regency.

Essential board games no house should be without (in no particular order):

Scrabble
You know: you make words and score points and stretch your little brain.

Boggle (see also Big Boggle, or Super Boggle)
More tiles – same idea: you make words, but against the clock and in any direction. I love this game – it's quick, it's cerebral, and children love the racing against the clock aspect. Very good for picking up new vocab. As with Scrabble and Snatch (below), have a dictionary to hand to avoid people having massive strops.

Snatch (from portobellogames.co.uk – arguably the best word game ever)
This is like the game you play with Scrabble tiles and no board. You
have a number of letters and make words out of them, which others
add to from their pile of letters, and 'snatch' from you – so CAT
becomes CART which becomes CARROT and so on. Addictive.

Cranium
Fantastic family game with different activities, from acting to
word games to sculpting things out of clay. Funny and riotous.

Apples to Apples
Great for bigger groups, especially bigger groups with mixed
ages. It's a comparison game, with cards, and a great deal
more fun than it sounds. Very simple – hardly any rules.

Perudo
Stephen Fry called this simple-to-learn dice game 'the second most
addictive thing to come out of South America' and he wasn't wrong. No
board, so super-portable, and involves bluffing, which is always a plus.

Backgammon
I used to supplement my student grant with backgammon. Hard to
describe – get someone to show you. Again, unbelievably addictive.

Mah-jong
I'm trying to learn so it's on the list – but it's not something you
pick up overnight, what with having to memorize the meaning
of dozens of tiles with Chinese writing/symbols on them.

Card Games

Essential card games: bridge, canasta, kalooki, poker. None of these are as complicated as they might seem, but you do need someone patient to teach you how to play. I'm not going to suggest you learn online, though you could certainly do so, because I have found to my (literal) cost that this is emphatically not thrifty; get a real person to show you instead. Simpler games, especially good for children: Cheat, Spite or Malice, rummy. *The Penguin Book of Card Games* (Penguin, £9.99), or a similar volume from your local library, will teach you hundreds more. Cards are the most brilliant fun – I feel desperately sorry for people who don't play.

Singing

Singing, via karaoke (see page 161), or round a piano or guitar, or with no accessories other than your voice. It sounds a bit von Trapp, and I'm not suggesting you dress your enormous teenagers in dirndl and force them to skip about singing, 'I am sixteen, going on seventeen', but there is something quite magical about a sing-song, even a drunken one. Singing really does lift the spirits (and if you like singing, join a community choir – your council will point you in the right direction. It's really good for you. I swear my mental health improved along with my lung capacity when I sang regularly).

Acting

Oh dear, now I really do sound like I have lost the plot. I don't mean putting on plays like a family of tragic ghastly thesps, though we did rent a house in Ireland one summer and amused ourselves (we had a new video camera) by writing, acting and filming a country house-style murder mystery. But if you have GCSE-age children doing Shakespeare, or a more contemporary playwright, spending a couple of evenings in comfy chairs, reading the play aloud, can really help them, and, nerdy as it sounds, it is quite good fun.

Film Evenings

The cinema, which I love, has become weirdly expensive when you consider the cost of tickets, plus parking, plus snacks, plus another snack on the way home. Which leaves the telly. I don't know about you, but I have a tendency to sit there like a potato, watching whatever inane crap comes on. This may be relaxing – well, kind of: I find it more stupefying than soothing – but it doesn't really nourish the brain or embellish the soul (on the contrary, some of the stuff I watch makes me want to have a bath). All this, coupled with the fact that my big children had no knowledge of the classic movies I loved as a child, has led to once-a-week film nights (with popcorn, which costs pence and takes minutes to make). It's a really nice way of spending time together, plus it's just bliss – you lie there in the dark in the comfort of your own sofa, snuggled under a blanket, watching *All About Eve*, or *Harvey*, or *Stand by Me*, and you go to bed feeling pleased because you've exposed your children to a little bit of painless culcha. Never buy DVDs – they're really expensive and they sit around afterwards taking up space. The online film rental clubs (like www.lovefilm.com) are very cheap and don't mind how late you are in returning your movie.

A Super-Easy Recipe for Toffee Popcorn

50g butter
50g caster sugar
2–3 tablespoons golden syrup

Put all the ingredients in a pan and stir continuously over a medium heat until the sugar dissolves. Don't turn the heat up too high or the mixture will burn and turn into treacle. Drizzle over a bowlful of home-popped corn. Yummy.

Reading

Obviously. Does anyone still spend the evening reading? I mean, I know individuals do – but there is something lovely about a whole group of people sprawled around, deep in their books, together physically but each in a world of their own.

Brilliant, Free Online Reading

These are some of my favourite wordy websites, in no order and on a variety of subjects, some clever, some inane (but funny). Every one of them is worth checking out.

* www.aldaily.com – or **Arts & Letters Daily**

A brilliantly selected pick of the best, most thought-provoking reading on the web, on every conceivable topic.

* http://gofugyourself.typepad.com

Mean, but beautifully written and often hysterically funny, dissection of celebrities' wardrobe malfunctions.

* www.lacoquette.blogs.com

Wonderfully readable blog by and about a young American woman living in Paris.

* http://jezebel.com

Celebrity, sex, fashion, books, politics and a great deal more, written for women by women. Provocative, brilliant, often very funny.

* www.fashionologie.com

Cool, knowing fashion blog.

* www.petiteanglaise.com

Catherine Sanderson's musings on life and love in Paris.

* www.timesonline.typepad.com/comment

Excellent, brilliantly compiled one-stop place for all the news, debate, opinion and current affairs you might want, not just from **The Times** but from all around the world.

* www.realclearpolitics.com

A must for anyone interested in American politics.

* www.thefirstpost.co.uk

Online daily magazine, covering everything from the depths to the shallows.

Online Magazines & Newspapers

All of the national newspapers are now online for you to read for free. Most of the weekly news magazines are too, though content may be limited. The **Economist** (.com) and the **Spectator** (.co.uk) both have excellent websites.

www.lrb.co.uk: the online home of the estimable **London Review of Books**. Subscribers get to see the whole thing online; ordinary punters still get a pretty good chunk of fortnightly reading matter.

www.harpers.org, www.mcsweeneys.net and **www.newyorker.com** are the respective websites of **Harper's**, **McSweeney's** and the **New Yorker**, all wonderful literary magazines (I find that such an off-putting and dry-sounding description – let's just say they're full of great and unexpected things to read).

www.salon.com and **www.slate.com** are both online magazines with no real paper presence; both contain quantities of excellent reading material.

The aforementioned **Arts & Letters Daily** (**www.aldaily.com**) is a repository of what it considers to be the best, or funniest, or most interesting or provocative writing on the Internet – it should be your first port of call once you've explored the more obvious places.

Eating

And, of course, eating. I don't eat with my children every night, and when we do eat together it's often in a bit of a rush. There is an embarrassment of evidence to suggest that the demise of the family meal is indirectly responsible for everything from horrible table manners to poor conversational skills to feelings of isolation and anger in older children. Try and remedy this regularly by making a delicious meal and sitting down together to eat it calmly and at leisure, and ask that the conversation centres around something interesting and adult. You may initially be met with some reluctance, but persevere and you will be rewarded. I don't see how children are supposed to form intelligent opinions about important topics like drugs, or gun crime, or immigration, or women, or what the various political parties stand for, if they never have the opportunity to discuss them outside of school lessons, or outside of chats with their peers. They also need adult input and a bit of robust debate. Also, it's nice to have children who aren't tongue-tied in adult company or, to be frank, embarrassingly dim about current affairs.

The Outside World

First point: window-shopping is not a pastime, nor an efficient use of 'leisure time' (where do these hideous expressions come from?) — not that that stops half the country from waddling around looking at handbags every Saturday afternoon. You could be doing so much more, much of it either free or cheap.

Walking and Cycling

Go for a walk. I know — yawn, what a boring suggestion. But it isn't really. Walking is fantastic (and so is cycling for that matter). It's good for you and good for your figure, your lungs, your heart and your skin. It is really soothing — after a while, all those little niggly irritations disappear. Walking (or cycling) on a beautiful day, through a beautiful park, can be wildly exhilarating. Walking in the rain has its own joys. Despite being bipeds, hardly any of us walk in any kind of serious way and I think this is a terrible shame, especially given the sedentary nature of many of our jobs. If we all went for regular brisk walks, none of us would be fat and we wouldn't have such a vast number of obese kids. Walking is also an excellent way of reminding ourselves that

the world is beautiful and full of interesting things. Which sounds
wet, I do see – but the wetness doesn't stop it from being true.

You don't necessarily need to walk aimlessly. If you have children in tow,
try a nature walk. If you've got to go to work, walk there, or part of the way.
If nature bores you (it bored me to death until I was about thirty-five),
walk through town – though the problem with this is that town walks really
benefit from you looking up at the buildings, which makes you bump into
people all the time. If you're in a new place, walk. Forget guidebooks:
walking is the best way of finding things out and making exciting
discoveries, whether they relate to a nice-looking pub, a blue plaque, a
garden full of hollyhocks or a family of ducklings you like the look of.

Talks and Lectures

Most large cities are heaving with free talks and lectures on a vast
number of subjects, from the sublime to the ridiculous. Avail yourself
of these: whatever you're interested in – baroque architecture, ghosts,
jam, dingoes, violas, Guyana, ungulates, Henry James – will be being
talked about knowledgeably somewhere at some point this week. By
and large, boring people aren't asked to give talks or lectures, which
means you are unlikely to have a dull time or to feel you've wasted your
evening. Feed your brain! Added advantage: unlike wandering about
aimlessly, or going to the cinema, or doing anything else that's familiar,
going to a talk really takes you to a completely different place in your
head – sometimes it feels almost like having had a mini holiday.

Museums

Museums aren't just for tourists. In fact they're not for tourists at all –
they're there for you, the residents. You don't need me to tell you how
utterly wonderful museums are – they feed your soul as well as your brain
– but you may nevertheless need a gentle prod in their direction. Use your
museums. I think many people underuse them because we have the idea

that a museum is a thing to walk around silently for the best part of a day, being forced to have intelligent thoughts. This isn't at all true – well, it can be true if you want it to be, but I find the best way of having a little culture hit is to use museums much as you use cafés: pop in for half an hour, go and look at one or two amazing, beautiful or curious things (such as the fleas wearing tiny flea-clothes at the Pitt-Rivers in Oxford: I mean, what kind of morning isn't improved by that?), then get on with the rest of your day. Few of us have the time to spend hours and hours lost in the British Museum, more's the pity, but we can all manage to nip in, be dazzled by the little faience blue hippo (Egyptian, 1850 BC!) or *Aphrodite Bathing* and nip out again. I'm always going to pay speedy visits to 'my' works of art in museums all around London and I heartily recommend you do the same, wherever you live (and including small, odd museums as well as the big ones). If you like museums, or if you want to grow to love them, invest in Mark Fisher's brilliant, magisterial *Britain's Best Museums and Galleries* (Allen Lane, £20), which is written with such cleverness and contagious enthusiasm that it makes you champ at the bit for your culture fix.

Libraries

I spent a disproportionate amount of my time when I was thirteen or so at the library (it was in Keats's old London house) and have loved libraries ever since. It's not just the content, or the smell, but the thrilling idea that you could read about anything at all in the whole world, and transport yourself to an almost infinite number of places in your head. If you're interested in something, whether it is prosaic or recherché, do by all means look it up online, but then go and spend a couple of hours reading about it at the library. It's so satisfying: you go in ignorant – virgin,

almost – and come out knowing stuff. I don't know how to convey my enthusiasm for libraries without sounding swotty. Swottiness is part of it, but there's so much more (and see pages 133–4). If you haven't hung out in libraries since you were at school, do give 'em a whirl.

Theatre and Concerts

Theatres are the opposite of cheap, but cheap tickets are available; your first port of call should be www.theatremonkey.com, followed by www. lastminute.com. Some theatres hold tickets to sell cheap on the day – check directly with them and be prepared to queue first thing in the morning. Then there are the ones that involve you peering out from behind a column – not ideal, I'll grant you, but still better than vegging out at home with a tube of Pringles. There may be discounts available for local residents, as well as for students and OAPs, and some theatres put on community productions, hold free workshops and so on. It's always worth asking, especially if your theatre is small and local. Remember also that pub and fringe theatre tickets cost a fraction of the price of West End ones. Pick judiciously and you may see a show that's headed Up West anyway.

Remember, the cheapest way to buy tickets to concerts, games and so on in general is to cut out the middle man: i.e. to buy direct from the venue. For concerts, it's worth checking with the band's fan club – joining it for not very much may entitle you to discounted tickets.

Want to go to a sold-out event? Scarlet Mist (www.scarletmist. com) is an ethical ticket exchange/buying website, where tickets trade for their face value – goodbye madly inflated eBay prices.

The Cinema

You know when yours sells its cheapest tickets. Some cinemas, such as the Prince Charles in London, always sell cheap tickets because they put on films later than the regular places. It is also possible to see free films: www.londonisfree.com/film will tell you where they're on in the capital. The British Film Institute lets you download a free film every month if you are a member. And don't forget you can get two-for-one tickets on a Wednesday by texting the word 'film' to 241 if you have an Orange mobile phone contract.

Get Out of Town

Sometimes a change really is as good as a rest. Visit some of these sites for inspiration:

www.nationaltrail.co.uk
Look up routes for walking or cycling through the finest landscapes in England and Wales.

www.nationaltrust.org.uk
Lots of amazing bits of countryside, coastlines and nature reserves to visit.

www.nts.org.uk
Same for Scotland.

www.forestry.gov.uk/website/fchomepages.nsf/hp/GBEEE
Find a forest to explore in your area and download various guides.

www.wwt.org.uk/centre/119/visit/wetlandcentre/.html
Explore the wildlife at London Wetland Centre at Barnes.

What Not to Scrimp On

Memberships to stuff. For example, it costs £15.40 a pop for one person to go to London Zoo, which is insane and prohibitive. An Adult Annual Pass, at the time of writing, costs £50 and you can go any time you like – ten times a day, every day, if the fancy takes you. We used to go to the Zoo once or twice a year as a treat. Now, thanks to our passes, we're there practically every week (we live nearby) – a quick nip to say hi to the tapirs and okapis, then home again. This principle applies across the board. If you like something and want to make maximum use of it, be thrifty and join its club.

Beauty

he **truth of the matter is**, genes have an awful lot to do with skin – much more than beauty companies give them credit for. You may be one of the lucky few who can abuse their skin horribly – never wear sunscreen, smoke like a chimney, get drunk every night, feast on chocolate and sleep in their make-up; if your mother and grandmother have fantastic skin, chances are you will too, regardless of what you do to it and how much you mistreat it. That's the first (unfair) thing to understand.

The second is that most of us don't have a genetic predisposition to exquisite skin and have to work for it a little bit harder. If you don't have naturally amazing skin and you regularly do any or all of the above, you'll pay, in wrinkles or spots or – wahey – both at the same time (a sort of teenage-granny look that is especially unappealing).

What I am trying to say is that it is absurd to claim that all beauty products are a swizz, as some people regularly do, but it is equally absurd to expect them to have magical results. People who have truly fantastic skin either have it anyway – they could be rubbing bacon fat on their face every night, for all the difference products make to them – or achieve it through having 'work' done.

Which leads me to fact number three: if you want magic, you're talking medical intervention. No over-the-counter creams will make adult acne disappear, but prescription drugs will. No wrinkle cream will leave you completely smooth-browed – that's Botox's job. If you have enormous pores, no potion will shrink them enough – you want a peel. If you have serious issues with your skin, I am (cautiously) in favour of these procedures.

I am also ENTIRELY AGAINST doing them on the cheap. Please, please don't. You will ruin your face and look like a freak. See a reputable dermatologist, one who is accredited, or see nobody at all: have a read of www.bad.org.uk/public/what/ for pointers. I'm just going to say it again, because I know of people who go and have toxins injected in their face by their manicurist or random beautician. For God's sake, don't. This is serious stuff and if it's to work it needs a serious, highly skilled doctor to administer it. Serious doctors don't come cheap and they have waiting lists. They are not thrifty, so we'll speak no more of them here, but I just wanted to get that off my chest, because the general 'Hello, random woman in spurious white coat and orange tan. Yes, do stick that needle into my face' trend really worries me. (All of this also applies to cheap cosmetic surgery. If you're going to get your tits done, you want an artist, not Coco the Clown. Seriously – what is wrong with people that they think it's going to be fine to get this stuff done at bargain-basement prices?)

Anyway, as I was saying, most of us require a little maintenance to keep us looking perky. The million-dollar question is, is there anything in the £100 face cream that there isn't in the £10 cream? Of course there is. Will it make a noticeable difference to you if you save up and start using the former? Not necessarily, no. Confusing, isn't it? I've come up in zits or blotches from ultra-deluxe tubs of cream I've been sent (as a journalist) to sample and had really good skin from sticking on a bit of cheap stuff in a pot I got at a hippie market because it smelled nice. The following observations are entirely personal, but they work for me and I don't see why they shouldn't work for you.

Skincare

If you want better skin – smoother, plumped, more even-toned, more elastic – drink water and plenty of it. This is the single best thing you can do: hydrate from within and flush away crap while you're at it. I know it sounds like an old magazine chestnut, I know you've heard it a million times, I know it's hard to imagine such a small, free thing could make a big difference, but it does. By the way, by the time your body registers thirst, you're already mildly dehydrated, so don't wait till you feel parched. It's really simple: if I drink masses of water, I have skin that looks ten years younger than it really is (on a good day). If I don't, I have thin-feeling, crinkly, papery skin with horrible dry patches.

If you want better skin, eat fat. I discovered this when I was dieting, which involved eating a mixture of (mostly) protein and 'good' fat, in the form of butter and olive oil. Fat appears to lubricate skin from within – I'm sure there's a more scientific explanation for it, but this is how I think of it. No fat: sad-looking, caved-in skin. Olive oil on my fish: boingy skin. QED. Another thing I really noticed when I was dieting: eating protein gives you stronger, shinier hair and nails.

The sun is very nice, but it eventually gives you the skin of an old crocodile, or a prehistoric beast. One day you're perfectly fine, the next your face is Fortuny-pleated. Wear sunscreen. Really.

Skin is porous – obviously – which means that whatever you put on it absorbs to an extent. The average woman applies 126 ingredients and chemicals to her skin every day; they come from everyday products such as soap, cleanser, toner, face cream, foundation, mascara, lipstick, eyeshadow, powder, shower gel, deodorant, body lotion, shampoo and conditioner.

Expensive face creams contain some or all of the following: petrochemicals, parabens, sodium lauryls and artificial colourings. Some are known allergens and some are known carcinogens. Yeah, yeah, you're saying – everything's bad for you. I know what you mean: life's too short. However, when you think about it, this is how it works out. On the one hand, we have posh, branded face creams, costing upwards of £30 per 50ml. They're loaded with all this bad stuff and they don't seem to work demonstrably better than cheaper creams. On the other hand, we have the natural/organic companies. Their creams start at around £15 per 50ml: i.e. half the price of the big brands. They use high-quality, predominantly organic (or as close as) ingredients and leave out the chemical nasties. Many of these natural brands regularly come out on top in surveys when real women try them out (as opposed to beauty professionals, who constantly sing the praises of every new expensive face cream in print. Why? Because they can hardly crap on their own doorstep by refuting the claims of their most valuable advertisers – i.e. cosmetics companies – and say X is worthless or Y is actively bad. I do wish women would realize this. Some beauty editors are better than others, but the entire publishing industry runs on advertising, therefore obviously their hands are tied to an extent when it comes to comment.* This is why websites, especially blogs and punters' review sites – addresses coming up – are so brilliant: they have no need for spin and just tell the honest truth).

* Funnily enough – or not – one of the best nearly organic lines, This Works, was founded by my sometime colleague Kathy Phillips, a former beauty editor of Vogue.

I Don't Understand Which Ingredients Are Creepy and Which Aren't

The brilliant Sarah Stacey and Josephine Fairley go into this in some detail in their **Green Beauty Bible** (Kyle Cathie, £19.99), and have also, thoughtfully, listed and explained all the ingredients that come up in cosmetics on their website. You can find the list here: www.beautybible.com/green_pages/ingredients-index.htm

So, expensive line full of weird, potentially dodgy stuff, none of which necessarily gives you better results, or cheaper line that is purer and works. Which would you rather use? It's not rocket science, is it?

Now, I'm sure there are wonderful, premium beauty creams and potions out there. And it is an absolute fact that what the giant brands are brilliant at is research, which they have the money to fund, though of course the research eventually trickles down to the smaller brands. What I'm still not convinced about is whether the poshos do a better job of making us look better than the cheap-to-middling brands (try them out: ask for free samples). And since this is a book about economy, and since the global beauty industry is worth about 100 billion, we're going to leave the top-end brands where they belong, which may well be on the shelves of gullible people with more money than sense. Or, if you want to put it more kindly, eternal optimists.

Olive Oil

Next question: what to use without breaking the bank? We'll start with the very basic and move up to the more treaty-feeling. I give you two words: olive oil. Yes, really. It makes a brilliant moisturizer (face and body) and it's full of polyphenols (antioxidants which slow the ageing process). Drawback: you smell like salad. Avoid this by mixing (good, cold-pressed, extra virgin) olive oil with rose water and a drop of lavender oil, or just slap it on when you're sleeping alone. To avoid the salad smell issue altogether, you can substitute almond oil. For more on how to wash your face with (home-made) oil, see www.oilcleansingmethod.com. It also works brilliantly as a treatment for dry hands – rub some in before going to bed and ideally wear a pair of cotton gloves on top (once it's absorbed – you don't want it all soaking into the fabric); and dry feet (ditto, except with socks). You can use it as a hair treatment if your hair is dry and desiccated-feeling: rub in all over, stick a tight bath hat on top (hello, sexy) or wrap your head in foil and leave on for an hour or so. Warm olive oil will soften cuticles as well as dry elbows, knees and feet. Put some in the bath to emerge soft all over (again, you may want to add a few drops of essential oils to avoid smelling like salad). You can even use it as shaving cream or lip balm.

I have great faith in oil generally and am especially fond of oil cleansers. These sound like a complete disaster if you have oily skin: oil + oil = hello, pizza face, you would think. But no. The oil takes everything off and dissolves on contact with water, so you're left totally clean (and soft) but not in a dry, stripped way (if you strip oily skin, it produces more oil to compensate. 'Tis crucial to keep it unstripped). All the premium brands have started doing cleansing oils (Shu Uemura did it decades ago – theirs are great, but very expensive). The cheapest good one I know of is DHC Deep Cleansing Oil, £16 for 200ml (www.dhcuk.co.uk). It is based on olive oil, which is good.

You don't want weird mineral (i.e. petroleum-based – nice) oils in your oil cleanser.

By the way, all cleansers can be removed with water – you don't need special foaming ones. If you like a cream cleanser, but also like the feel of water on your face, rinse it off. Makes no difference. It took me ages to work this out.

Homemade Beauty Products

Up a bit from slapping on stuff that you normally reserve for the rocket, make your own products. I know this sounds like taking thrift too far, but I've been making some myself in the name of research and do you know, they work. Well, I say 'making' – they're really simple. This is what I've done:

Used oatmeal as an exfoliator. You get into the shower with some porridge oats, basically, all Scottishly. Take a handful, dampen it, scrub yourself like mad, do it again if you like, rinse off, and lo! You're all soft. Nice smell, too.

This is when I was trying to copy a sugar scrub that cost £30 a pot. Get into the shower with some sugar in a plastic bowl. Same principle, except you mix your sugar into a stiffish paste with a bit of olive oil so it doesn't just fall off; I added a drop of geranium oil, so it smelled nice. Scrub, rinse, result: you're all soft again.

I've also tried the same principle with salt, both normal and Epsom, and it works very well. I slightly believe in the magical powers of Epsom salts, which are magnesium sulphate – apart from anything else, if you have an Epsom salts bath you come out weighing less; in my experience, the salts appear to temporarily draw out bloat. It's not especially good for you, I don't imagine, but it's mighty handy every now and then if the dress you want to wear is on the tight side and you have to leave the house in half an hour.

Apple cider vinegar makes your hair shiny. I don't know why. I just put a couple of glugs on my hair after conditioning but before rinsing.

 Smearing your face with good-quality honey and leaving it on for about fifteen minutes gives you even, super-soft skin.

Smearing it with yogurt (which contains lactic acid, which is like AHAs) works well if you need to exfoliate.

You are going to thank me so much for this one. It's not for dry or sensitive skin, but if you're oily or combo or even acne-prone, rejoice. It's the aspirin mask, which I discovered years ago while browsing on the utterly genius www.makeupalley.com, one of my favourite sites of all time. MUA is a repository of everything to do with beauty and has tens of thousands of online reviews of products, from skincare to scent. These reviews tell it like it is: always try and have a read before buying the new so-called must-have potion. But anyway, the aspirin mask. The idea is that aspirin contains salicylic acid, aka BHA, or beta hydroxy acid, which is the main component of all of those majorly expensive designer exfoliators/creams, as well as of many an acne treatment. Cost of said products: upwards of £40. Cost of aspirin mask: pence. Get six aspirins – plain, uncoated aspirins. Crush them with the back of a spoon. Mix with a bit of water to make a paste. Put the paste on your face. Leave it there for ten minutes. Rinse off, massaging to exfoliate as you go. For God's sake keep your mouth and eyes shut. Pat face dry. Open eyes. Look! Your skin looks about a million times better and your blemishes are dying. Note, though, that BHA is strong and you can't go slapping it on willy-nilly. Use once a week, twice in an emergency. Exfoliated skin is sensitized: use sunscreen. Use a mini-version of the aspirin mask on isolated spots. They will die, and it's a lot cheaper than spot cream.

There are hundreds of home beauty recipes online.
Try the following for starters:

www.makeyourcosmetics.com
Gives you recipes and sells you ingredients.

www.beautyden.com/beautyrecipes.shtml

www.spaindex.com/HomeSpa/HomeSpa.htm
Recipes for the face, body, lips, hair, hands and feet and the bath.

www.allnaturalbeauty.us/hbr_mainpage.htm
Lots of great recipes, categorized by ingredient.

www.honey.com/consumers/sb/videos/blueberry/blueberry.html
Video showing you how to make a honey and blueberry facial.

www.teachsoap.com
Learn how to make soap, as well as lip balms and lotions.

www.brambleberry.com
Soap-making supplier.

Buying Beauty Products

Now, actual products. Since I don't know what your skin is like,
I'm listing brands rather than specific lotions. All of the following
come highly recommended, are fine to use on sensitive skin, don't
contain anything weird or dangerous, and won't break the bank.

Green

Dr Hauschka: *www.drhauschka.co.uk*

Spiezia Organics: *www.spieziaorganics.com*

- **Liz Earle:** *www.lizearle.com* (wonderful line that really does the job for about half the price of posher brands; really highly recommended)

- **Weleda:** *www.weleda.co.uk*

- **Lavera:** *www.lavera.co.uk*

Not Green, but Still Great

- **Cetaphil:** brilliant, super-cheap cleanser you get from your chemist

- **Dr Nick Lowe's line, available from Boots:** he is an excellent dermatologist and the products are entirely affordable; great cleanser, £9.95

- **Olay's moisturizers** (the cleansers are too harsh)

- **Boots No. 7 range:** totally up to speed on the research and development front and much, much cheaper than their multinational counterparts

Make-up

Now we've got the skin sorted, let's put on some slap. Expensive make-up is lovely – it looks nice, it's nice to play with, the compacts are satisfyingly heavy and make sonorous clicks when you open and shut them, the lipsticks look sexy in their golden cases. But is expensive make-up going to make you look better than cheap make-up? No. It's make-up, for heaven's sake – it washes off at the end of the day. If your eyeshadow doesn't stay on for twelve hours because it cost £2 instead of £20, put some more on when you go for a wee. It's hardly the end of the world, is it?

I was going to write, when I was planning this book, that you do need to spend money on foundation. Nobody wants a bad colour match, or a chalky-looking face, or anything that makes you appear caked in make-up. I still think that holds true if you use traditional foundation. Pay for the best, the best in my view being Prescriptives Custom-Blended Foundation, which is like your own skin, but in a bottle – you can literally put it on in the dark. Armani is excellent as well. You also want some Laura Mercier Secret Camouflage, which remains the world's best concealer.

But then – tadaa! – I discovered mineral foundations. I can honestly say that these have changed my life, in a small but significant way. For a start, they're incredibly cheap – and they last forever. I'd been aware of them for a while before trying them, but had discounted them on the basis that they were powders and would therefore never give me the amount of coverage I wanted. Not that I have monstrous skin, but I do like it to look pulled together on the foundation front, not like I've just stuck on a bit of powder. Then I went to New York and was told that the number-one-selling foundation in America is Bare Minerals, by Bare Escentuals. I was quite surprised: it looks like feeble powder. I also had several girlfriends who were using mineral make-up and swore they would never go back to the liquid stuff. They looked great, and they made all sorts of extravagant claims about how good the make-up had been for their skins – no blackheads, no breakouts, no weird red bits for no reason.

Mineral foundation is basically ground-up minerals and pigments, specifically titanium and zinc oxide, both of which occur naturally and provide an SPF of 15. Zinc has anti-inflammatory properties (hence its use in nappy cream) and is particularly good for conditions like rosacea and acne. Minerals are non-comedogenic – i.e. they won't block pores – and are great for people with allergy-prone skin. They are pretty much water-resistant. Best of all, there's nothing dubious in these products at all – no waxes, oils, chemicals, artificial colours or preservatives.

Bare Escentuals claim that you can sleep in theirs; several plastic surgeons suggest you wear mineral make-up after surgery, such is its purity.

Well – everything is true. Mineral foundation is amazing stuff. It gives you almost airbrushed-looking skin and covers every bump and shadow. It stays on all day, even if it's boiling hot. It doesn't look or feel like you have anything on. And my favourite brand of all, the stupidly named Lily Lolo, is so cheap that it's almost like a joke: at the time of writing, a little jar of it, which will last you months and months, costs £12. I like Lily Lolo (www.lilylolo.co.uk) because I think its colours are excellent, particularly if you have yellow-toned (rather than pink-toned) skin, because it's cheap as chips and works brilliantly, and also because its dazzling eyeshadows and blushers are the business (you need a minuscule amount). Other excellent mineral make-up brands are Jane Iredale (considerably more expensive) and Bare Escentuals (mid-range; theirs are called i.d. bare minerals). Note that everyone's trying to get in on the minerals act, and bigger companies are now launching their own mineral lines. Approach with caution and read the label. The whole point is that these products are natural, but some companies are choosing to add oils, talc, waxes, fillers, colours, preservatives and other chemicals to theirs. I'd stick to the three brands I've named, personally. Note also, mineral foundation may not be your cup of tea if your skin is exceptionally dry. And it's all in the application with mineral foundation – it took me a while to understand this. Watch a demo online by putting 'mineral foundation' into YouTube's search engine.

Everyone loves a personal beauty recommendation and the goodness of the Internet is that it's packed full of them. Your first port of call should always be the aforementioned www.makeupalley.com (though be warned – it's horribly addictive). The following beauty blogs/sites are all fantastic; some have fashiony bits too. As ever, they will lead you to hundreds more through their links:

www.blogdorfgoodman.blogspot.com
Wonderful, aesthetically pleasing fashion/
beauty blog with masses of tips and advice.

http://allaboutthepretty.typepad.com
Comprehensive blog, which also rounds
up other blogs, usefully, containing lots of reviews of products.

www.beautywriter.blogspot.com
The blog is, appropriately, called 'Champagne taste on a beer budget'.

http://thebeautybrains.com
Answers readers' questions in reassuringly authoritative manner.

www.hey-dollface.com
Lots of reviews, tips and advice.

www.megsmakeup.com
Unbiased beauty products reviews: what works, what doesn't.

www.beautifullybookish.blogspot.com
Librarian by day, beauty addict by night.

http://jezebel.com
Has an occasional anonymous and brutally honest beauty column written
by someone who works at Sephora, the giant make-up/skincare emporium.
It's pretty enlightening.

Make-up is about the raw ingredients, yes, but it's mostly in the
application. It's just as easy to go wrong with a Chanel eyeshadow as it is
with a Superdrug one – which is where online make-up demonstrations
come in so handy. There are masses of these all over the web; either
VideoJug or YouTube.com (which has tens of thousands of make-up
tutorials) is a good starting point – just do a search. Once again,
www.makeupalley.com has a whole dedicated make-up board, which offers

lots of information as well as great advice should you wish to achieve a particular look. I'm amazed by MUA's make-up board: some of the girls on there are true artists. With the information on the blogs, on MUA and via the make-up tutorials online, you could give yourself a new look every day until you were 100. This isn't even an exaggeration. Get out there, or rather get online, and play with your face. Make-up can completely change your look – and I mean completely, to the point where an acquaintance wouldn't recognize you in the street. It's really only one down from surgery. Now, with all the resources available on t'interweb, anyone with a bit of time and a steady hand can become an expert, for free and in the privacy of their own home. You'd be mad not to give it a go.

Buying Make-up

You pay for packaging first and content second. Chanel make-up is a great deal more expensive than Bourjois make-up, even though Chanel and Bourjois are owned by the same company, just like Lancôme is owned by L'Oréal (a lot of elite posh brands make stuff for less posh, or even budget, own brands. Carlsberg is reputed to make Asda Smart Price beer; Glenmorangie bottle most of the supermarket malts, Aiwa is part of Sony, and so on and so forth).

Having said that, there are obviously differences between high-end and low-end make-up. But only sometimes.

- **As I was saying, buy mineral make-up – the whole cosmetics expense/results issue is sorted in one fell swoop**. If you don't like it (you will), buy expensive foundation, as above, in small bottles – it turns after twelve months.

- **Remember that make-up doesn't have a long shelf life** – you're supposed to chuck it after a few months (three for mascara, to avoid eye infections) for hygiene reasons, but also because it dries out.

It is pointless to spend money where you don't need to. Powders have longer shelf lives because they have no water content in which germs can breed (another good reason to go mineral. I'm sounding obsessed, aren't I? It's because I am).

🌸 **Eyeshadow doesn't have anything to do with price and has everything to do with pigment**, which gives the colour its depth. It's a question of trial and error: get a sample, put it on and see how true the colour on your skin is to the colour in the pan. MAC eyeshadows are heavily pigmented; any other brand with the word 'pigment' in the product's title is likely to be a good bet. However, if you like neutrals, buy them cheapissimo. Nude eyeshadow is nude eyeshadow – you don't need a heap of pigment for the natural look.

🌸 **This is also true of blusher** – but actually, I prefer weedy blusher to a really strong one, because it's easier to add to the colour than to remove it. Ergo, cheap blusher is great.

🌸 **Cheap lipsticks aren't – the colour seeps and fades**. If you like strong colours, don't buy the ultra-cheapies. If you like neutrals, go ahead.

🌸 **But do buy super-cheap drugstore lipgloss**. It's lipgloss. It comes off and you reapply it. Don't pay through the nose for the privilege. Also, remember Vaseline – cheap as anything and lasts forever.

🌸 **You don't need eyebrow pencils**. Dark eyeshadow looks far more convincing.

🌸 **Brushes**: the really cheap ones are rubbish because they moult or are so stiff they scratch your face. The high-end ones don't make any difference application-wise and are a rip-off. Go for the mid-range, such as (again) MAC.

Nail polish chips, no matter how grand the brand. Buy cheap polish, but invest in a good top coat to prolong its life. If you're worried about the chemicals in nail polish (an unbelievable amount), check out brands such as Butter London (www.butterlondon.com).

Mascara: I have to say, my three favourites are expensive (Dior Show, Sisley and YSL Effet Faux Cils). They do look like you're wearing falsies, though. 'Green' mascara doesn't work – you need the horrible chemicals to make the stuff stick to your lashes. I've never met a really cheap mascara that impressed me, but Max Factor Lash Perfection (mid-range) is terrific.

Eye pencils: the cheaper ones are marginally harder. Warm them in your hand, or with your breath, or with a lighter (for a nanosecond). I don't see the point of expensive eye pencils.

Lipliner: there's quite a lot to be said for wearing only lipliner all over your lips, with Vaseline on top – it lasts forever and looks very natural. In which case, once again, pigment is your friend.

Liquid eyeliner: you don't get what you pay for. I wear this a lot and have at one stage or another bought every brand going (and used my daughter's black face paint in extremis). The most tenacious – as in you can go swimming, bake in the sun all day, have a shower and go out again, and it won't budge – are MAC (I wish they sponsored me) and Bobbi Brown gel eyeliners. Both are old-school: i.e. you apply them with a brush. 2True from Superdrug is only marginally less good, and cheap.

❀ When you're bored with your make-up, swap it, either with friends or online. There's a hyperactive swapping community at www.makeupalley.com. Compare your list of haves with their list of wants and away you go – free make-up. I wouldn't advise swapping used lipsticks or mascaras/eye pencils because of hygiene concerns.

But make-up is only make-up – it's sweeties for the face. Devoted to it as I am, I no longer lurk like an addict round the capital's beauty halls. I'm just as likely to be found trawling the cheapy teenage ranges at Boots, or at the absolutely wonderful Elf, where everything costs £1.50 (www.eyeslipface.co.uk). My make-up bag is now tiny – titchy little pots of multi-tasking mineral make-up that do everything. All of the fun, but none of the guilt – I recommend it.

How to Kill Spots

We're always told that it is a heinous crime to attempt to do this ourselves and that it will leave us with terrible pitted, scarred faces and destroy our lives. I'm sure this perhaps applies if you have chronic acne (in which case, Google 'acne diet'; it basically involves restricting carbohydrates, which really don't do anybody any good at all, as far as I can see, and works for a lot of people).

However, if you have normal skin which occasionally breaks out in a mild way, or if you get spots at the time of your period, you can absolutely deal with them yourself, without the expense of a facialist.

Do this at night, as follows:

🌸 **Wash your hands very thoroughly and cut your fingernails.**

🌸 **Clean your face using your ordinary cleanser and warm water.**

🌸 **Get a magnifying mirror.** Take your lenses/glasses off if you're short-
    sighted – you'll see your skin better. Stand close to the mirror in good
    lighting (light from above is the cruellest. Handy re spot-killing, less
    so in restaurants on hot dates. If you're in a restaurant on a hot date
    and there is a spotlight above your head, beaming down, ask to move).

🌸 **Identify the culprits.** Don't go overboard – you're after obvious
    lumps or bumps, not after every minutely blocked pore.

🌸 **You know what to do**: squeeze gently and persistently,
    using a clean bit of tissue. Gross . . .

🌸 **This is the important bit**: you now have clear pores,
    but they're irritated and all big and gapey. You want to
    wash your face again, with cold water this time, and
    immediately apply a clay mask – any clay mask, including
    the ones that come in little sachets and cost under £1.

🌸 **Go and lie down for ten minutes.**

🌸 **Take the mask off** with a cloth and tepid water.

🌸 **Moisturize**, but not the T-zone.

🌸 **Go to bed.**

🌸 **Wake up with much clearer skin**
    and normal-sized pores.

How to Look Expensive

Some people sort of exude luxe, even if they're wearing jeans and a T-shirt, and some people can spend a fortune on their clothes and make-up and still look somehow scruffy, or like they're playing at dressing up (I'm one of the latter. I like to think it's by choice). I've been interested in this since I was about twelve – what is it that makes X look so polished and Y look so rough, even though X's disposable income is a fraction of Y's, who has regular facials and weekly manicures? These are my conclusions:

🌸 **Very important point to grasp: looking expensive doesn't have anything to do with looking sexy.** It has to do with looking clean (of course, some people find clean = sexy, just to confuse matters). So, no bed hair, no obvious lipstick, no smoky eyes, no clothes that suggest you might have walked home in them first thing this morning. Nothing obviously tight, no dangly earrings or statement jewellery, no fishnets. Shoes: small heels or flats.

🌸 **Looking expensive is mostly to do with good skin**, both on face and body.

🌸 **It's therefore also a question of make-up**. Looking expensive means immaculate, impeccably applied (as in invisible) foundation: you want to be smooth, even, tiny-pored. Your face needs to look clean and like you're not wearing anything on it. Minimal blusher, long shiny eyelashes, bit of lip gloss, nothing shouty.

🌸 **But all of these things need to be really well applied** (even if it takes an hour to look like you spent five minutes), otherwise you just look like a normal person without much make-up on, not like an heiress tramping the streets incognito.

🌸 **It's also to do with eyebrows, which need to be perfectly tweezed**. Too thin is common, too bushy is scruffy, too arched is draggy.

🌸 **You need to be perfectly groomed**. Shiny, clean hair, which isn't doing anything too elaborate. Short, squoval nails, au naturel or with neutral polish, on hands and feet. No body hair – stubbly legs don't look expensive and the curlicued armpit is repulsive in any context. Depilate within an inch of your life.

🌸 **You need to be quite shiny**. Matt looks poor rather than luxey – chalky rather than blooming. Moisturize. Drink water. Use a dab of illuminating cream on your cheekbones and round the edges of your face.

🌸 **You want to look prettily flushed rather than like you're wearing blusher**; the best way of achieving this is with a liquid cheek tint (cheap, plus lasts forever. You can make your own with glycerine and grated beetroot; there are recipes online).

🌸 **Your skin can be either alabaster white or tanned**. Exfoliate like mad – you don't want any dead or dry skin anywhere, because it looks really grotty. Then either keep out of the sun or use one of those progressive fake tans, the cheap ones that come as body lotion, unless you're brown in the first place.

🌸 **Clothes: less is more.** Wear really well-cut basics in neutral shades, with the odd pop of colour (my problem is that I dress like a parrot). Neutral colours – biscuity-coloured things, navy, white, deep black – look expensive even if they're cheap in a way that reds and pinks do not. Wear graphic prints rather than flowery or mad ones.

🌸 **Beware of monochrome** (black and white), despite what magazines tell you. It's a hard look to pull off unless your clothes are very chic. Blokes in cheap

suits and nylon shirts are technically doing monochrome
– enough said. Cheap black (see page 67) is especially
horrible; you might be better off sticking with navy.

 Wear white shirts and spray them with starch
before putting them on.

 Beware the 100 per cent man-made fibre.
There's nothing chic about giving off static.

Keep legs as natural-looking as possible: no 'fun' tights
– opaques in winter, bare brown legs in summer.

You need one smart handbag, which will make
an enormous difference. Nothing blingy, nothing
It-ish, nothing that is the shape *du jour* – but
something classic and luxurious-seeming in black
or brown. This kind of handbag is a sound investment,
because you will literally use it forever. Don't buy
knock-offs – they look like knock-offs. It doesn't matter if your bag
is from a market stall, as long as it's handsome and unobtrusive.

You can get away with cheap shoes, provided they look expensive.
This usually means a) fairly plain and b) lovingly cared for – polished,
stuffed with newspaper after they've been rained on, etc. (see page 70).

Small jewellery, unless you are fat, in which case small jewellery will
look absurd. Either way, you want unobtrusive, 'good' pieces (or cheap
approximations of them).

Your hair mustn't look obviously dyed, which is easy if you are blonde,
less so if you are dark. Hair dyed black makes everything look cheap – go
for lighter-than-your-natural-hair-colour streaks that could look as
though the sun has lightened parts of your hair.

🌸 **TEETH! Very important**. Grotty teeth are a complete no-no. You may not be able to afford home-bleaching kits or trips to the laser clinic, but you can ensure your teeth are sparkling white. If you smoke or drink tea or red wine, the best way of doing this is by using an electric toothbrush. For my money, the Philips Sonicare range is impossible to beat – they lighten your teeth by a couple of shades and make you look like you live at the hygienist. They are not cheap, but they last forever and I personally feel they are essential. Spread the cost: any number of people can use them – just buy extra heads.

Colouring Your Hair

You don't always need to spend a fortune having your hair coloured at the hairdresser's. Obviously, home hair-colouring is much less expensive (a box of hair dye usually ranges from £5 to £15, whereas in the salon colouring usually costs £35 and up, depending on the method used and the length of your hair). That doesn't mean it's always the solution. Nobody wants to look like a freak, even if the process was marvellously cheap. Remember that a cock-up with the home dye can mean you end up paying for the dye itself plus the (salon) cost of fixing it. My advice is, proceed with caution.

Leave your hair in the hands of a professional if:

It is severely damaged.

You want to lighten it more than three shades or do something drastic like go from blonde to black or vice versa.

You've already coloured it, you screwed up and you want to fix it.

Otherwise, there's no reason at all why you shouldn't give it a go yourself.

Choosing Dye

First of all, make sure you use a
popular brand of hair dye — popular
brands are usually popular for a reason.
If Clairol's hair products turned your hair
green, you'd know about it.

Secondly, there are two different variables
to consider when buying a home hair-colouring
product: the colour commitment and the actual colour.
If you're dyeing your hair and want to go for a dramatic change,
it's best to get the professionals involved (at least for a consultation).
Otherwise, stick to a shade within a few of your natural colour. If this
is your first time colouring your hair, it's probably best to start with
a low level of commitment, then (if you're happy with the results)
you can work your way up the commitment ladder. It's kind of like
the difference between first base and yer actual grope. The following
are the most common commitment levels used by most major product
lines, ranked in order from the least committed to the most.

Semi-Permanent Colour

The best choice for hair-dye virgins. Colour washes out after about
six to twelve shampoos. They don't contain any ammonia or peroxide
(but this generally means you won't be able to lighten your hair any
shades, only add colour).

Demi-Permanent Colour

Demi-permanent products last longer than the semi-permanents
(approximately twenty-five shampoos). They also contain no
ammonia, so you can't use them to lighten your hair, but a small level
of peroxide allows you to create a more noticeable colour change.

Highlighting

Highlighting at home? Don't bother, unless you want to look like a slightly gingery badger.

Permanent Colour

Permanent colour uses both ammonia and peroxide, which cannot be washed out, so if you don't like the results, your only options are to wait for it to grow out or dye over it. Keep in mind that the end result is always a combination of the added pigment and the original pigment of your hair, so the dye may look different on you than on the model on the box.

Hiding Grey Hair

If your hair is less than 20 per cent grey, it's best to use a semi-permanent colour that is one shade lighter than your natural colour to allow the grey to blend in. If your hair is more grey, permanent dye is really the only way to completely cover the unwanted colour.

Tips for When You Dye Your Hair

Make sure you do both a strand test and an allergy test before you begin the dyeing process (instructions for how to do this will come with the product).

Although home hair-dye kits are easy-peasy to use, you should still take care to keep the dye on your hair and nowhere else, so: always wear gloves (which should come with the product). Wrap an old towel around your shoulders to protect your skin and clothes.

To limit chemical contact with your skin spread a thick layer of Vaseline around your hairline, over your ears and down the back of your neck where the dye is most likely to meet your skin. Any dye will slide over it and wash off. (If your skin has been dyed, rub in toothpaste, which miraculously takes the colour away.)

VERY IMPORTANT: NOW FOLLOW THE INSTRUCTIONS ON THE BOX AND MAKE SURE YOU READ THEM AT LEAST TWICE! Different products have very different instructions and you don't want to find you were supposed to begin with dry hair halfway through applying the dye to your freshly washed locks.

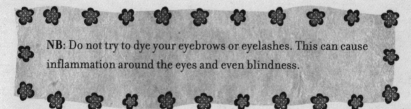

NB: Do not try to dye your eyebrows or eyelashes. This can cause inflammation around the eyes and even blindness.

Fixing Mistakes

If you're not happy with your new hair colour, don't sit at home in a state of depression. Get down to the hairdresser's, where they have a variety of techniques to fix colour cock-ups.

Maintaining Your Colour

General tips:

 Chlorine can strip or dull your colour, so wear a cap if you're going swimming in a pool.

Frequent washing with harsh shampoo can also strip your colour, so use mild shampoos designed for coloured and treated hair. You also need to make sure you condition like mad.

The sun can oxidize your colour, so protect your hair by using a leave-in conditioner during the summer and wear a hat when you go on holiday.

Root Touch-up

Hair colour should last up to eight weeks before your roots begin to show. But instead of dyeing the whole thing again, just touch-up the roots with one of the many home kits you can buy at the chemist's. Clairol Nice 'n Easy Root Touch Ups is one of the best.

Natural Hair Dye

Most permanent hair colorants contain a fairly nasty mixture of peroxide and ammonia. There is now a growing market for more natural hair-dyeing options which are less damaging to hair and less toxic to the body, although they are less effective than their more toxic cousins. If you're worried about dirty chemicals, try one of the following companies, which specialize in more natural products that don't contain as many nasty ingredients:

www.danielfieldmailorder.co.uk

www.tintsofnature.co.uk

www.herbatint.co.uk

Henna

Henna is a natural colorant derived from the henna plant. It's been used to dye skin and hair for centuries. It's also been a hippie favourite for some decades. Personally, I love the look it gives. What's more, it's really good for your hair and makes it super-shiny.

Although it is completely natural, it is permanent and can have quite drastic results. If you don't like the results, you can't dye over it with ordinary hair dye but only with another henna product, because henna coats the outer hair shaft, affecting the penetration of the chemical colorant. This coating of the outer shaft is how henna makes your hair gorgeous and shiny, but it's also why it's a complete nightmare to remove.

General tips:

Make sure you do a strand test.

You must wait at least six months after dyeing your hair with a chemical colorant before using a henna dye (or your hair might turn green).

Make sure you buy your henna from a reputable company. Lush do some lovely henna hair bars that look like impressively geometric poos: www.lush.co.uk (Lush also do excellent, by which I mean resulty as well as wholesome, face creams, by the way – don't be put off by the fact your twelve-year-old daughter likes hanging out in there).

Do your research: www.hennaforhair.com.

Massage

Complete heaven, but so expensive. Solution: learn how to do it yourself (though not, alas, to yourself – it's never very satisfactory). Therefore, learn with at least one other person, so that you can practise on each other. You can put someone's back out by just rubbing it vigorously willy-nilly, and semi-cripple them by trying to walk along it, so don't. Amateur massages work best on heads, shoulders and feet, as well as legs, arms and hands. There's a selection clips at VideoJug showing you how to carry out various kinds of massage. Make some time, make some space, dim the lights, get comfy and away you go. You'll need oils – a carrier oil and an aromatherapy one. Good oils to use as carriers are sweet almond oil, apricot kernel oil, jojoba oil, fractionated coconut oil and sunflower oil

(see? You don't even need to buy it – it's in your kitchen).
Olive oil would work too. Sesame oil is used in Ayurvedic
medicine, but it smells of stir-fry – if you want to use
either of these, blend them with a lighter oil and add
fragrance via essential oils.

Essential Oils

You're either into these or you aren't. Some people
swear by them as cures for anything and everything.

If you are going to buy essential oils, quality is paramount. Even an oil
which is quite truthfully described as 'pure' may be of poor quality and
therefore of less value therapeutically. Essential oils are concentrated
aromatic plant extracts collected through a process of steam distillation.
If the oil is cheap, it may be a third or fourth distillate from a batch of plant
material which has already yielded the greater part of its properties to the
first or second distillation. There's not much point in using it, really.

As a rough guide, look for simple but informative labelling (botanical
name, part of plant), avoid any oils that are not packed in opaque
glass and don't buy anything that seems like a bit of a bargain.

Young Living (www.younglivingeurope.com) sells a range of top-quality
oils online. They're not cheap, but they last a long time and are delicious.

Some good essential oil/aromatherapy websites:

www.aromatherapypoint.com/essentialoils
A comprehensive list of essential oils and
their therapeutic properties.

www.naturesgift.com/methods.htm
Loads of ways to use essential oils.

🔖 *www.quinessence.com/methods_of_use.htm*
Ways to use essential oils to energize and uplift your home.

🔖 *www.care2.com/greenliving/uplifting-essential-oils-8-ways.html*
More of the same.

Mooncups

I can't write about the question of personal upkeep and thrift without mentioning these. Brace yourselves, cos it ain't pretty. However. You know periods? And how it costs an absolute fortune to buy Tampax, or sanitary towels, or Lil-lets, and how this monthly expense is somehow more irritating than many others? (I really mean this. What do poor people do? Tampax should at least be tax-free, and I think free entirely for women living on benefits.) Well, here's an ultra-budget solution.

Now, I'm not going to lie and tell you I've personally tried this out. I just can't get my head around it. I'm on perfect speakers with my vagina – Lordy, what a sentence to write – but I am one of those people who is repulsed by the idea of non-applicator tampons, on the basis that they're . . . messy. I mean, I'm sorry – if I have my period, I don't want to emerge from the cubicle and really desperately need to wash my hands, if you know what I mean. Not when Tampax, or other applicator-ready protection, exists. Whenever I mention this to people – it's a marvellous ice-breaker at cocktail parties, at the opera, at corporate events and so on – my girlfriends tell me I'm a freak and that they have no such issues.

Perhaps I am a freak; certainly I find non-applicator sanpro revolting. If you are similarly inclined, the Mooncup is not for you. But if you don't care about a bit of honest womanly menstrual blood on your hands, read on.

Mooncups are internal vessels that gather your menstrual fluid, and which you empty, wash and reuse. They stay in via the goodness of suction. I know – they sound like the ultimate hippie accessory. However, they are reportedly one of those life-changingly brilliant things, and are used by all kinds of women, captains of industry as well as yoga teachers. These women say Mooncups – diggin' the name, man – are superior to Tampax for the following reasons:

- **They work brilliantly and never leak.**

- **They are environmentally sound** because you only need one (they don't fill up landfill sites or the oceans like tampons and sanitary towels).

- **They are made from a special medical-grade non-allergic silicone** (silicone is derived from silica, which is one of the most abundant minerals on earth) and so do not cause irritation and are suitable for women with sensitive skin, thrush, eczema or allergies.

- **They last for years.**

- **They are a much healthier option** in that they do not suck moisture out of you, leach pesticides into you or deposit fibres on your vaginal wall (now there's a pretty image).

So there you go. Read all about them at www.mooncup.co.uk; you can buy them online and also from Boots, for around £20. I can't emphasize enough how people, even people with very heavy periods and weary pelvic floors, rave about these – they really are evangelical about them. Here's an email from a friend about hers: 'You are MAD not to try one. They have literally changed my life, from a week of paranoid misery and worry about leaks to barely noticing I have my period.'

What Not to Scrimp On

Medical procedures, including surgery. Foundation. Bright lipsticks.
Really good haircuts. A decent hairdryer, with a diffuser if you
have frizz issues. Hair products that work for you if you have tricky
hair – but do remember that some of us grew up in the days before
conditioner existed and still had shiny, healthy hair; and also that hair
product overload can result in seriously bad hair days – keep it simple.
As for serums for frizzy hair, a drop of oil works (I use jasmine hair
oil from Indian grocers), and so, in extremis, does Vaseline or body
lotion. Nevertheless, my unruly, curly hair would be a mess without
Kérastase's incredible Oléo-Curl range (Aveda's Be Curly products
come a close second), which isn't cheap but means I can finally do
my own hair and make it look nice – goodbye, blow-dries; hello,
hundreds of pounds a year saved.

Don't scrimp on scent. I don't believe in cheap perfume, but far more
expert people than me do: world-class noses make scent for big
brands as well as niche ones, after all. I'm a snob about scent, and
I'm probably wrong to be. Among others, www.perfumeoflife.com,
www.perfumeposse.com and http://nowsmellthis.blogharbor.com will
enlighten you. I am obsessed with scent, and scent blogs, some of
which have given me greater pleasure than almost anything else I've
read online. Google 'Luca Turin' to see what I mean. And remember
you don't have to buy the whole bottle – buy decants on eBay, or
swap for them at www.makeupalley.com.

ranted, it's never been cheaper to go abroad. And, sometimes, go abroad you must – it wouldn't do at all to become all weird and insular and turn into one of those people, like a sometime relative, who once literally wept with disgust at the idea that people might want to go to horrid fancy foreign France in the summer when the bounty of 1970s Britain was on their own doorstep.

Nevertheless, I have become quite passionate about holidaying in the UK. To be honest, this doesn't really have as much to do with my concerns about my family's carbon footprint as with expense and convenience. If you're a single person with a decent income, or a couple, the world is your oyster and travelling is usually straightforward and manageable. If you have small children in tow, though (to say nothing of a neurotic dog that needs parking somewhere), the whole thing can very quickly become a particularly stressful way of leaching money. To make matters worse, you sometimes get the sinking feeling that the fun doesn't seem worth the cost.

The problem is partly that an adult's idea of a blissful holiday abroad very seldom coincides with a child's. Say I want to lounge scenically around Tuscany (just to be especially clichédly middle class about it). I rent, at vast expense, a villa to lounge in. It's really nice for me – I like the food, I love the heat, I like Giotto, I love churches, I speak Italian, I like swimming and lying in the sun, and not having a telly is my idea of heaven.

For my children, only two of those pronouncements are true – those concerning food and swimming. The rest bores them to tears. And, as I have discovered over the years, there's only so much swimming you can reasonably expect a child to do in a fortnight. The pool is massively exciting for the first three days, after which you find children in various stages of mild disenchantment (which immediately puts you in a filthy mood – what kind of hideous brats have you raised that they turn their noses up at pools and olive groves?). Why don't you go for a swim? you say, slightly aggressively. I swam all morning, they say, and now there's nothing to do. Go for a walk. No, it's too hot. Also, I'm fifteen. I don't want to walk through the countryside looking at flippin' trees. Well, do something, you roar. We haven't come all the way out here and practically bankrupted ourselves for you to lie around like a slob. And no, you can't play Gameboy. You play Gameboy in London. We are on holiday. It is special.

Meanwhile, the baby has got a rash and you're wondering if she has heatstroke, despite spending the day unhappily smothered in a thick coating of Factor 50 (she's fractious anyway because she didn't sleep last night, because it was too hot), and the middle one's been stung by one of the many wasps that congregate at mealtimes in the charming outdoor loggia. Never mind, you explain, because this afternoon we're all going to climb a clocktower. We'll have an amazing view of the whole of Siena. And later I'm going to drag you all around town, in the broiling heat, until we find a church I went to when I was twelve, which contains an especially interesting relic. It'll be such fun!

Or not.

Deciding to give British holidays a whirl was the best decision I ever made. It saved me thousands of pounds but, even more importantly, it provided us with holidays we could all enjoy. Nobody has to be at Heathrow at an ungodly hour, in horrible crowds, to find delays and disgusting breakfasts that cost a tenner a head and are swimming in grease. Nobody screams throughout the flight because their ears aren't popping. Nobody has difficulty finding the car hire place, and then gets lost for four hours finding the villa. And that's just for starters.

Instead, you just get in your car and go. You stop off at a nice family-friendly pub for lunch. You take your time. You arrive, and everything's exciting but not too unfamiliar. The sea is turquoise. The sun is shining – and if it isn't, it will at some point. The beach is huge and pristine. The fish tastes like it walked out of the sea ten minutes beforehand and the chips are crispy. The children aren't forced to bob about in a swimming pool for a fortnight: they can bodyboard, they can surf, they can fish, they can go on boat trips, they can look for seals, they can go crabbing, the big ones can go off by themselves and explore the nearest town, the little ones can check out the rockpools. In the evenings, the big ones can hang out with other teenagers, while you put the baby to bed, pour yourself a glass of wine and admire the sunset. It is bliss.

Yes, it does sometimes rain. So what, really? You read your books, you play your board games, you eat massive dinners, you put on waterproofs and go out anyway. There's always something to look at and something to explore. What I also especially like about these holidays is their old-fashionedness. There will be plenty of time to explore Las Vegas, or the Amalfi Coast, or Zanzibar, but meanwhile we're all here in Cornwall, and it's a bit Famous Five and comical, but nobody's being spoiled with deluxe holidays, nobody is developing a sense of entitlement about deserving to only go to flash places and our entertainment isn't linked to the need to spend money. We're doing small, ordinary things, albeit extremely enjoyable ones.

Accommodation

Accommodation is, obviously, key. Here is some advice for getting yours cheap.

Location

Be fussy about location, but not about aesthetics or star ratings. I've rented some extremely expensive properties in the past which had posh kitchens and nice bathrooms, but were miles away from the beach and therefore a complete waste of time – the idea is not to spend ages in the car if you feel like an impromptu pre-prandial dip. Then I realized the error of my ways and started renting physically unattractive (grotesque, even), dramatically cheaper – because you pay a premium for wooden floors, madly, but not for incredible views – bungalows that were either on, or across from, the beach (this is all in Cornwall and Devon). OK, so they're never going to win design awards, and the swirly carpet isn't necessarily your cup of tea – but so what? Last year's jewel was next door to a beach café that did surfing lessons and organic breakfasts, to say nothing of jugs of Pimms at sunset. We had candlewick bedspreads, a beige plastic kitchen, hideous strip lighting and an embarrassment of 'art' on the walls featuring big-eyed children with cloth caps, but it was fantastic: you could be on the beach in one minute flat and every night the sunset was like a painting.

Beach Chalets

If you prefer something prettier, have a look at beach chalets, which seem to me to be the best of all worlds: affordable, nice, on the beach. You could start here, to get a rough idea of what to expect: www.stives.co.uk/st-ives-beach-chalets.htm.

Also, www.beach-huts.com will find you a beach hut – cottage, really – big enough to stay in for much less than the price of a 'real' house (from roughly £400 a week for one that sleeps four), or a smaller one to rent to keep your beach stuff in for the duration of your stay (from £80 a week). Saves humping windbreaks, deckchairs, mallets and inflatables up and down the beach.

Caravans

Do not discount the static caravan. They're absolutely brilliant – I'm saving up to buy one in Camber Sands as I write, but you can also hire them. I started noticing, a few years ago, that many caravan sites were absolutely brilliantly located, often very near the smart house we'd paid a fortune to rent, and often closer to the beach than said smart house – one, I realized with a pang of sheer envy two years ago, backed right on to the dunes. Have a look at www.static-caravan.co.uk to find yours, and check out Haven Holidays, once unkindly described as CenterParcs for chavs (and me):

www.havenholidays.co.uk. Their bookings have gone up by 30 per cent year on year at the time of writing, as a direct result of the credit crunch. I say crunch or no crunch, these are brilliant, cheerful family holidays and your children will love them; last-minute deal prices start at around £385 for a static caravan that sleeps eight for a week. (This also applies to Butlins. I'm mad about Butlins. When I say to people, 'Please, I beg, take me to Butlins for the weekend,' they laugh and think I'm being cutely ironic. I'm not. I *love* Butlins – everything about it puts me in a good mood.) At Haven, look out for the sites which have a David Bellamy Conservation Award, which they get by proving their commitment to 'preserving and enhancing the natural world'. Some have wildlife trails, interpretation centres, children's activities and wildlife events. If you're used to paying through the nose for your nice smart house, you'll get a very pleasant surprise.

Do also check out www.ukparks.com, which will find you a caravan park featuring statics to rent wherever and whenever you want to go.

Do not discount the caravan-caravan either, or the noble motorhome. Again, sales and rentals are going through the roof at the time of writing and it's not hard to see why: you get all the benefits of being away with none of the prohibitive accommodation costs, and if you don't like Place A, you just drive to Place B. Go to www.campingandcaravanningclub.co.uk to be pointed in the right direction.

If you're a fashion stylist and the thought of caravans pains you, try a Romany caravan (such as the ones here: www.new-forest-gypsy-caravans. co.uk), which would cost a family of four about £375 for one week. Then there's www.underthethatch.co.uk, which has gypsy caravans in Wales for £329 a week.

Camper Vans

If you fancy those wonderful 1960s VW camper vans, which you can sleep in as well as scoot about in, www.scoobycampers.com is one of the many companies that will rent you one (refurbished). Prices vary, but roughly speaking a family of four would spend about £325 renting one for a week.

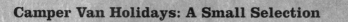

Camper Van Holidays: A Small Selection

* **www.isleofwightcampers.co.uk/index.asp** (based in the Isle of Wight)

* **www.cotswoldcampers.co.uk** (based in the Cotswolds)

* **www.oconnorscampers.co.uk** (based in Devon)

* **www.southcoastcampers.com/home** (based in Dorset)

* **www.sevendegreeswest.co.uk/home.asp** (based in Bristol)

* **www.roomwithaview-camperhire.co.uk** (based in the Lake District)

* **www.coolcampervans.com** (based in Derbyshire)

* **www.kirarentals.co.uk/en** (based in Scotland)

Camping

And then, of course, there's camping, which has never been cooler or more popular. There also now exist family-friendly sites with play areas and luxury bathrooms, yurts with four-poster beds and roll-top baths, and hireable 'tents' that are really more like cottages. For great advice on finding the right campsite for you, or for hiring a caravan, have a look at the amazingly comprehensive www.timesonline. co.uk/tol/system/topicRoot/Camping_and_caravanning.

Feather Down Farms are a brilliant invention. They're camping, but not as we know it. The 'tents' – which have solid wood floors and sturdy canvas walls – live in fields on various organic farms all over Britain; you don't have erect anything. *Au contraire*, these babies have comfy beds (with hay duvets), a flushable loo, a cold chest and even a wood-burning stove. The living area is 45 square metres: i.e. massive compared to a normal tent. And the Feather Down ones are beautiful – like something out of a movie about 1930s bohemians. You get your food from the farm you're staying on; there's no hot water and no electricity, but each farm has a wood-fired oven for pizzas and chickens for organic breakfast eggs. Children love these places and parents do too. Tents sleep six and cost from £345 a week in low season. Very highly recommended – see www.featherdown.co.uk – and there is now a Feather Down in France.

Also, discover the joy of yurts. Most yurt-hire companies are into saving the planet and have lots of ideas for nice gentle activities to do in their corresponding areas. There is also usually organic food somewhere nearby, if it's not growing in the field next door. Yurts are absolutely wonderful and really comfy. On average, a yurt sleeping four would cost around £300 a week, but prices vary depending on the time of year and the location. Here are some good companies:

Cornwall

 www.plan-itearth.org.
uk/yurt-holidays.html

www.yurtworks.co.uk/
holidays/index.htm

www.southpenquite.
co.uk/yurt.html

www.adventurecornwall.
co.uk/yurt.htm

www.cottageholidayscornwall.
co.uk/yurt.html

Cumbria

www.rainorsfarm.
co.uk/yurtindex.html

www.lake-district-yurts.co.uk/

Derbyshire

www.ambervalleyyurts.
co.uk/index.htm

Devon

www.yurt-holidays.co.uk/

 www.devonyurtholidays.
co.uk/yurts.html

www.blackdownyurts.co.uk/

Dorset

www.yurtvillage.co.uk/

Gloucestershire

 www.theorganicfarmshop.
co.uk/produce.htm

Herefordshire

woodlandtipis.co.uk/index.php

Wales

www.broomeretreat.co.uk

www.downtoearthproject.org.uk/

www.trellyn.co.uk/index.html

www.annwnvalley.co.uk/index.htm

www.home.clara.net/
trallwyn/trallwynyurt.html

www.larkhilltipis.co.uk/yurt.htm

House Swaps

Try a house swap. Your urban pad – avoiding the prohibitive costs of urban hotels – may be a more attractive proposition for someone than you could possibly imagine, even for people who appear to live idyllic lives by the seaside/deep in photogenic countryside. Use the home swap places (see below) but remember that it is also worth approaching holiday home owners you find online directly to ask them if they'd be interested in a swap. I've done this twice, with great success (by email and enclosing photographs). Ask, and you shall receive.

Anyway, house swaps are an invention of genius and can be hugely successful, providing you with a fantastic holiday anywhere in the world at bargain-basement prices. There are a few ground rules:

The main one is DON'T LIE when describing either your house or your neighbourhood. If you live in a nice area but it borders a rough one – pretty much a given in many urban places, including London – say so. If your neighbourhood is rough but your neighbours divine, say so. If you're trying to swap your flat for an apartment in New York, your potential swappees will know exactly what you're talking about and won't be put off. But they will, rightly, be extremely annoyed if you make Tottenham sound like Mayfair, then they discover it isn't quite so once they've travelled thousands of miles.

Don't exaggerate the virtues of your house. Don't do it down either, but do be honest. If the wi-fi doesn't work on the top floor, say so, rather than saying the house is fully wireless. If the bicycles you're leaving for your swappees' use are functional but ancient, tell them. If you live under the flight path, let them know.

Try and give a sense of the neighbourhood. Saying it's nice for families, or whatever, isn't enough. Try and paint a portrait – the delicious smoothies available round the corner, the great secret picnic spot in the local park, the café/shop/restaurant situation, the friendliness of your neighbours, the good public transport links, the fact there's a school nearby and things are noisy between 3.30 and 4 p.m. and so on.

 Communicate as much as possible. Send pictures, of course, but don't be shy of asking any questions you may have, no matter how numerous or nitpicky – and don't get stroppy when people do it back to you.

 Don't assume that what you see as a disadvantage can't be viewed by a potential swappee as a virtue, and vice versa. If your local garden square is overrun with toddlers at the weekends, that may be annoying for sunbathing singletons but great for young parents. If your local pub has a late licence and jazz nights on a Thursday, it may annoy a lover of peace and quiet but sway a night-owl music fan. If all your restaurants are ethnic, that could be a foodie's idea of bliss; if they're all greasy spoons, they might please a chronic Anglophile. And so on.

The websites you need are:

* *www.homebase-hols.com*

* *www.homeexchange.com*

* *www.homelink.org.uk*

* *www.gti-home-exchange.com*

Don't forget the micro-holiday, also known as the weekend house swap. Basically, you swap houses with a friend from Friday to Sunday – a friend who lives out of the way, not the friend in the next street, though I suppose that could work too. That's it. Free, completely easy and works especially well if you have children who are the same sort of age, because they can play with each other's toys.

Other Useful Travel Information

- **www.seat61.com** will show you how to travel cheaply round Europe by boat or train.

- **www.sidestep.com** is the best travel comparison site by miles – key in your details and it'll search 200 travel websites to bring you the cheapest fare.

- **www.daysoutguide.co.uk** lists off-peak fares, offers and free attractions.

- **Book train seats as early** as you can to ensure the cheapest fare – twelve weeks early if possible.

- **Get a railcard (www.railcard.co.uk)** if you are a frequent leisure traveller – they typically cut a third off the fare (but check the small print re travelling times).

- **www.nationalrail.co.uk** has a promotions and special offers page.

- **www.megatrain.co.uk** can enable you to travel along certain routes for £1 provided you book early enough.

- **First-class dining carriages**, where they still exist, are open to all classes of ticket holders and don't usually kick you out after you've finished eating.

- **Sleeper trains are romantic**, efficient and save on a night's accommodation costs.

- **www.moneysavingexpert.com/travel/cheap-train-tickets** has some nifty tricks, involving buying, say, four tickets instead of one for the constituent parts of the same journey – you can save an awful lot of money by doing this.

What Not to Scrimp On

It's difficult to be authoritative about this, since the question of whether you value accommodation over transport method, or whatever, is so subjective. So, subjectively: I personally wouldn't scrimp on accommodation, especially within the UK, when the weather is likely to prove unreliable. Staying somewhere ultra-basic makes no difference if you're out gambolling in the sun all day, but it can be a bit of a bummer if it pours with rain for a fortnight and you have nowhere comfortable to sit.

Do take out holiday insurance. Nobody ever thinks they're going to need it, but people frequently do and being abroad without insurance in the case of an accident can be prohibitively expensive.

Location: the best bargain in the world isn't actually much of a bargain if it takes you two hours of sitting in traffic to get to where you really want to be. So, pay extra to put yourself in exactly the right spot – you'll save on petrol, overheating and stress.

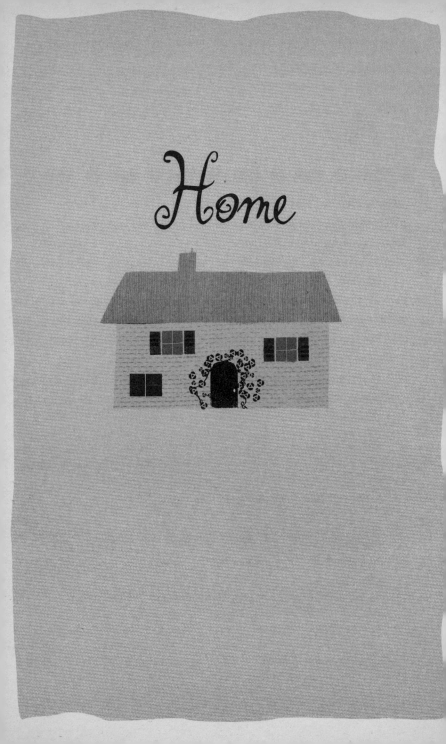

*Y*our home. Your nest. Your roost. The idea here is to make it so wonderful that you never want to leave it, thereby saving yourself a great deal of money.

We've seen how you can fill it with the delicious smell of home cooking, how you can recline on home-made cushions fashioned out of old jumpers, how you can turn it into a crafting paradise, a board-game sanctuary or a poker palace, how you can make money out of your new-found love of crochet, and shop for bargains online, how you can have great cheap nights in with your friends and a cocktail shaker. We're going to start this chapter with a few less romantic but nevertheless necessary ways of saving money on your home, while greening it at the same time – I shan't pretend it's terribly exciting, but I do think it matters.

Energy

The first thing you might want to do is to assess how efficient your home is in terms of energy use. It's an unsexy thing to kick off with, but sorting this out can make a major difference to your fuel bills, and assuage any concerns you may have about not doing your bit planet-wise. You may have to pay out to get the insulation sorted or the windows secondarily glazed, but the long-term advantages for both the environment and your pocket make it really worthwhile. The following websites can help you figure out what you need to do – you fill in an online questionnaire and they then tell you how much energy and money you could save, and how you go about it:

www.energysavingtrust.org.uk

www.britishgas.co.uk//energy-efficiency.html?WT.seg_3=i100049

www.greenlivingonline.com/Energy/8-energy-saving-renovations-
for-your-home

I could at this point go into minute details about how to cut your utilities bills by switching suppliers, etc. but, frankly, there are entire websites devoted to this, of which the best is our friend www.moneysavingexpert. com/utilities.

Household Recycling

(see also pages 128–30)

- **www.recyclenow.com** gives recycling advice — it tells you what can be recycled and how to go about it.

- **www.recycle-more.co.uk** has copious general information.

- **www.greenlivingonline.com** has good advice about broken appliances, like whether to replace or repair them, among a slew of other useful articles.

- **Go paperless with all your bills.** Not only does it help trees, but you will no longer have to navigate through reams of paper. No more boring bill mail either. Most companies offer a paperless option; many give you a little discount for choosing it.

- **Register with the Direct Marketing Association** (www.controlyourpost.co.uk) and with the Mail Preference Service (www.mpsonline.org.uk) to put an end to junk mail.

- **See the information on Freecycle** on page 129.

Cleaning Products

We are all supposedly being poisoned in our own homes by our daily reliance on powerful and toxic detergents (which we then rinse away into the water supply, poisoning everything else). To avoid this, making your own cleaning products is easy, pleasing and cost-effective. Plus you can wipe down your surfaces without having to make babies and infants leave the room first, or giving yourself a coughing fit. Plus it works. Plus it's really cheap and doesn't give you weird rashes on your hands and arms, unlike many a cleaning product I could name.

A common ingredient in the following recipes is borax, which is a very safe substance (it turns up in some cosmetics, not that that's any guarantee) with low toxicity for humans. It's a highly effective anti-bacterial, cleaning, fungicidal and bleaching agent, and is a safe and healthy option both for you and for the little ole planet. You can get it inexpensively from Tesco and Boots.

❀ **Make your own floor and carpet cleaners**: www.creative-home.net/Article64.htm.

❀ **Make your own laundry soap**: www.creative-home.net/Article67.htm.

❀ **Make your own surface cleaners**: www.creative-home.net/Article62.htm.

You can also use a mixture of borax and bicarbonate of soda (1 tablespoon of each) to make your own dishwasher powder. There are dozens of uses – it makes fine china shine brilliantly, for instance – and many of them are listed at www.dri-pak.co.uk, which will also sell you all the old-fashioned cleaning materials, such as bicarb, borax, vinegar, soap flakes and soda crystals.

Vinegar is also an excellent, green alternative to many of the chemicals used for cleaning. You can use it to remove calcium build-up in kettles; to clear blocked drains; to clean metal; to get rid of fruit flies; and to remove various stains from clothes and from surfaces. For the full list of the hundreds of household uses you can put vinegar to – and it really begins to look like a miraculous product – go to www.vinegartips.com, which also has sections on cooking, automotive and pet care and gardening.

Soda crystals – no phosphates, enzymes or bleach – were pretty much the only domestic cleaners at the turn of the twentieth century. They need to be diluted in water – half a cup to 500ml water – and you want to wear rubber gloves if you're really sloshing it about. They're very good at cutting through grease and limescale, so work well at cleaning bathrooms and kitchens, and they clean ceramic or vinyl tiles (but strip the varnish off wood – use a borax solution instead; there are directions on www.dri-pak.co.uk and via Google). Wiping slatted blinds down with a soda crystal solution will clean them brilliantly and stop them getting so dusty next time. They can also be used to treat wine, ink and grass stains, and for a whole slew of other household tasks.

I'd just like to say that all of these things actually work, and work really well. I'd read about the quasi-miraculous properties of vinegar before, and knew that soda crystals did cool stuff, but I'd always suspected they couldn't possibly achieve proper results, as in the kinds of results you get almost instantly with chemical-laden cleaning products. Having now tried them, I see I was wrong. Using these more natural cleaning methods works beautifully and is extremely cost-effective. Add to that the fact that they aren't endangering your health or your family's (or pets'), and that they mean you don't live in a massively sanitized, over-deodorized environment (I have many theories about how living in too chemically clean a home triggers allergies, which I shan't bore you with here). It's a win-win situation, really. Do give them a go. And use them with rags – whatever happened to rags? – made from old T-shirts or clothes.

Composting

Reduce your domestic waste and do your garden some good. Here's how:

🌸 **First you need to decide what type of bin you want to use and whether you want to compost garden or kitchen waste or both**. Visit www.greengardener.co.uk to get some advice on what would suit you best.

🌸 **Place your bin on a level, well-drained spot** to allow excess water to drain out and make it easier for helpful creatures to get in and get working on breaking down the contents.

🌸 **Like any recipe, your compost relies on the right ingredients to make it work**. Good things to compost include vegetable peelings, fruit waste, teabags, plant and grass cuttings. These are called 'greens' and are quick to rot and provide important nitrogen and moisture. Other things you can compost include cardboard egg boxes, scrunched-up paper and fallen leaves. These are called 'browns' and are slower to rot but provide fibre and carbon. Crushed eggshells can be included to add useful minerals.

Don't compost cooked vegetables, meat, dairy products or diseased plants.

 The key to good compost lies in getting the mixture of 'greens' and 'browns' right. If your compost is too wet, add more 'browns'. If it's too dry, add some 'greens'.

 After approximately six to nine months your finished compost will be ready. It should be dark brown, almost black, and soil-like. Spreading the finished compost on to your flowerbeds greatly improves soil quality by helping it retain moisture and suppressing weeds.

See www.recyclenow.com/home_composting/composting/index. html for loads of useful information on home composting.

Worms

A wormery performs the same job as a compost heap but uses worms instead of bacteria and micro fungi. It is a smaller and more compact option and on a domestic scale works faster than a compost heap. It doesn't smell bad, so you can put it outside the back door, near the kitchen. Anything that has lived and died can be composted by worms, but the best results are obtained with soft organic waste such as vegetable peelings, tea leaves, coffee grounds, stale bread, pet hairs and even vacuum cleaner dust. Wiggly Wigglers, www.wigglywigglers.co.uk, is one-stop wormery heaven.

Gardening

I'm not going to give you a gardening lesson, especially as I can only grow things in pots (which I consider a minor triumph, actually), but the following site has advice and information about gardening that is kind to nature: www.english-nature.org.uk/Nature_In_The_Garden. It's also worth mentioning that populations of some English birds are declining rapidly (especially house sparrows, starlings and song thrushes). Gardeners can help prevent this by planting deciduous trees, native shrubs and climbers like honeysuckle or roses that can provide food and shelter for birds, and by allowing patches of grass to grow long, which means that insects thrive which means that the birds don't go hungry. I personally think everyone should let the grass grow and turn their garden into a mini-meadow: it looks beautiful, is helpful to creatures (and attracts butterflies) and children love it. The Royal Horticultural Society (www.rhs.org.uk) has information about how you'd go about doing this; www.reallywildflowers.co.uk sells you everything you need to start your own wild flower meadow, as well as providing masses of advice.

Some other useful websites:

www.rspb.org.uk/youth/makeanddo/activities/birdfeeder.asp
How to make a recycled bird feeder.

www.care2.com/greenliving/make-easy-bird-feeders.html
How to make a pine-cone bird feeder.

www.patriciaspots.com/birdbathhowto.htm
How to make a flowerpot bird bath.

Decorating

Painting

Painting is the quickest and cheapest way to give your home a new look.
I'm always really amazed, watching property or decorating programmes,
when potential buyers come into a room, immediately go, 'Ooh no, I
could never live with those yellow walls,' and huffily walk out again, as
though paint were an unshiftable geographical feature, like an active
volcano. Also, painting a wall is not difficult, though there are a few things
you should bear in mind if you want the result to look professional:

Don't just start painting – wash the walls down with sugar soap first.

Check for cracks or dents, then fill them in with filler, let
it dry and sand it down so it's all smooth and even.

Paint like a painter, not like a slapdash student. Have a look at
www.helpwithdiy.com/painting/painting_interior_walls.html, and
again at VideoJug to be shown rather than just told how to do it.

Don't paint only walls – small items of furniture get new leases of life
with a fresh coat of paint. For the shabby chic look, use two colours on
top of each other and attack them with wire wool once they're dry. It is

pathetically easy to do this even if you are really cack-handed and you'd pay through the nose for such an item in a trendy shop.

Label any leftover paint with the colour and the room it is used in.

To stop it drying out, cover the tin with a layer of cling film, put the lid back on securely and store upside down.

Don't throw unused paint away if you don't want to keep it. According to Community RePaint, last year 400 million litres of paint (retail and trade) were sold in the UK. Of this, it is estimated that 56 million litres are unused or just thrown away – enough paint to fill twenty-two Olympic-sized swimming pools. If your old paint is useable, donate it to Community RePaint (www.communityrepaint.org.uk) – enter your postcode and they'll tell you where your nearest donation point is. In 2006 the organization redistributed over 208,000 litres of paint (which otherwise would have ended up in landfill) worth over £800,000 to a total of 11,000 individuals and community and voluntary groups.

Painting Safely

Keep the room well ventilated and consider using eco paints.
There are concerns over the toxicity of standard paints, some of which
contain VOCs (volatile organic compounds), which are petrochemical
based solvents and can contain benzene, toluene, white spirit and xylene,
among others. They can cause headaches, allergic reactions and health
problems in the very old, very young and those with chronic illnesses.
If in doubt, ask your paint supplier, or look on their website.

Concerns about air pollution and hazardous waste have greatly
reduced the use of oil-based paints (which contain high amounts of
VOCs and toxic solvents). Water-based paints are much safer, but
some still have high levels of VOCs.

The good news is that these increasing health and safety concerns
have resulted in many paint manufacturers cleaning up their act;
great strides have been made in formulating paints that have no
or low VOCs and that still provide excellent results.

You can also choose from a range of eco paint brands that use
natural ingredients such as oils and clays as their base – especially
good if you have concerns about damp. The permeable clay paints
allow your walls to breathe and prevent the trapping of moisture
– perfect for older, solid-walled houses. They can also help to balance
the humidity levels in a room, as they can absorb and release moisture,
which prevents damp and mould developing. And of course they have
almost no odour. These eco paints are more expensive than regular
paint, and thus not thrifty money-wise, but I do think they compensate
by being thrifty on both the green front and the health front, especially
if you are painting children's rooms. You could use the cheapest paint
you can find, but it would arguably be the decorating equivalent of
feeding your child Turkey Twizzlers – a false economy, I feel.

For some nice brands of environmentally friendly paint, see:

www.thelittlegreene.com
English Heritage colours as well as groovy brights, all
deeply pigmented for excellent coverage (not a given, with
some greener makes: always try samples first)

www.auro.co.uk

www.earthbornpaints.co.uk

www.ecospaints.com

www.nutshellpaints.co.uk

I should also mention the brilliance that is blackboard paint, which
you get from www.plasti-kote.co.uk or any large DIY shop. You spray it
on to any flat surface and, hey presto, you have a blackboard, to draw
on or use as a giant Post-it note, or to write menus on or whatever.

Wallpapering

This is fiddly and difficult to do yourself, though not impossible – again,
look for instructional videos on YouTube and VideoJug. Nice wallpaper is
expensive. Where you can save money is in the materials you use. Basically,
you can stick anything up on the wall with wallpaper paste, so don't limit
yourself to expensive rolls of ready-made wallpaper. If the material you
are using is fragile, protect it once it's up with a coat of clear varnish.
Even materials that seem slightly cheap when they're on the kitchen table
benefit tremendously from being on the wall, all smooth and perfect. I'm
not suggesting you wallpaper your sitting room with sheets of the Financial
Times, but for smaller rooms consider using some of the following:

Sheet music

Maps

Wall charts – my playroom, or rather my daughter's, is papered in free nature charts that came with a newspaper and looks beautiful. (Plus I feel she's learning stuff by osmosis.)

Photographs from magazines – *National Geographic* for a nature lover, say, or Italian *Vogue* for an embryonic fashionista. Using pictures from magazines as wallpaper gives a completely different effect from pinning them up, or using Blu-tack – it looks very sleek and polished.

Collages – go all Joe Orton and spend a couple of evenings entertaining yourself by creating outré scenarios from existing pictures.

Posters – my teenage sons' bedrooms are wallpapered with posters and look fantastically cool rather than grottily studenty. When they go off someone – Eminem, wherefore art thou? – you just paste the next hero on top.

Wrapping paper – some of the wrapping paper being produced is incredibly beautiful and it seems a shame to use it, reuse, then chuck it. Use it as wallpaper instead.

Posters – as in grown-up posters rather than gloomy portraits of the Pigeon Detectives. I don't really believe in framing posters – it seems to defeat their intrinsic posterishness and make slightly too much of the fact you once saw a Rousseau exhibition at the Pompidou, but they look sort of vulnerable if you just pin them up. Use them as wallpaper instead – all those exhibitions you loved, all the plays you went to see, all the bands you loved in your youth, all the funny and/or charming posters you picked up abroad and don't quite know what to do with (those otherwise slightly hackneyed retro French posters for things like absinthe, cocoa and the Moulin Rouge look brilliant used to paper a whole kitchen wall).

These are just suggestions. Anything made of paper that's not uselessly thin or too thick and heavy can be slapped on the walls.

 www.betterwallpaper.co.uk will turn any photograph into a huge piece of wallpaper; www.55max.com will also do this, or turn it into a blind.

If you're very savvy on the computer graphics front, you can do this yourself (the wallpaper, not the blind). See http://blog.wired.com/geekdad/2007/05/last_year_we_de.html.

More wall ideas:

Investigate decoupage – see www.decoupage-online.com – and don't discount stencils as only being part of that whole late 1980s sponging/fleur-de-lys scene – you can get stunningly beautiful ones from the Stencil Library (www.stencil-library.com).

Upload a digital photo or picture and then go to http://homokaasu. org/rasterbator. They will convert it to whatever enormous size you'd like for free and send the enlarged version back to you as a series of PDFs. You then print and assemble like a puzzle, or mural. Perhaps not so environmentally friendly (if it all goes horribly wrong you could end up wasting a great deal of paper) but quite cool.

Furniture

New furniture can be crazily expensive – I must say, I don't entirely see the point of it, unless we're talking fitted kitchens (in which case go to Ikea – if it's good enough for the former editor of *Wallpaper**, it's good enough for you). The mass-produced stuff that isn't crazily expensive usually looks cheap, because it is. The only sensible solution, it seems to me, is to buy a judicious mix of expensive classics, hand-made stuff and second-hand.

The expensive classics needn't detain us over-long. You need the best bed you can afford and a comfortable sofa or two (always try out sofas and beds for at least fifteen minutes. I've sat and lain on some super-chic, aesthetically divine numbers that would guarantee anyone years of chronic backache).

A few general tips:

 If you need a specific item of furniture, always check out Freecycle (see page 129) first. People get rid of all sorts of stuff, from stinky nylon numbers to B&B Italia. The trick is to check frequently, not to have one little look and then give up. If you're after nice furniture, join groups in affluent areas: kind-hearted rich people are more likely to Freecycle something quidsworth.

Visit www.preloved.co.uk, where you can buy, sell and place free adverts for any second-hand item imaginable, including second-hand furniture.

www.iswap.co.uk has a furniture section – as the name indicates, it's a swapping site.

As is www.swapz.co.uk.

eBay is obviously a major player here – it's time-consuming, but there are serious bargains and finds to be had.

Familiarize yourself with your local junk shops and antiques markets, and always make a point of visiting new ones when you're away from home. Wonderful stuff turns up in the most unexpected places.

Architectural salvage: www.lassco.co.uk, www.coxarchitectural.co.uk and www.salvo.co.uk are absolute treasure troves, especially, but not exclusively, in terms of reclaimed flooring. Don't assume they're only good for huge stuff, like fireplaces – they often have fantastic door furniture, like beautiful knobs and switches.

 See pages 131–2 for car boot sales.

 Antiques markets, fairs, shops and flea markets: see www.antiques-atlas.com, www.antiquefairs.co.uk, www.theantiquesdirectory. co.uk, www.ukfayres.co.uk and www.antiques-web.co.uk.

Tip: don't shop for antiques or junk in prosperous towns with large down-from-London weekend populations on Saturdays or Sundays – the prices will have been raised to match the clientele's wallets.

Second-hand furniture shops are the one place where haggling is expected.

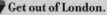 **Always check out antiques warehouses**, usually in unprepossessing buildings on the edge of town. They don't have the romance of dawdling in the sunshine somewhere scenic, but they yield great bargains.

Get out of London.

 If the shop is small, ask if you can see the warehouse/storing space and have a look at what they have in there.

If you're looking for something specific, offer to buy it cheaper with a cash discount, as it comes: i.e. before they've tarted it up. This applies especially to old kitchen tables and desks – in London they wire-wool them and wax them and charge you an extra £300.

If you don't like the colour of something made of wood, you can very easily stain it, either with wood stain or with Bri-Wax. Again, this is what the shop does and charges you extra for.

Caring for Your Things

This may seem an obvious point, but TLC prolongs the life of objects. In this disposable age, we're all too keen on consigning something to the bin/attic/recycling because it doesn't work any more, or because it's 'broken'. I feel it's really worth taking an evening class in basic electrics/DIY, because we should all be able to mend a broken lamp – but if you're not time-rich enough to sit learning, find someone to show you how or teach yourself online.

Ways of keeping your things looking lovely:

 Feed wood. It gets thirsty and it dries out. Furniture polish doesn't really cut the mustard after a while: you need wax, wire wool and elbow grease.

 Feed leather. It also dries out and cracks, plus it can fade. A good leather conditioner applied with a soft rag will keep things looking lustrous and pliable.

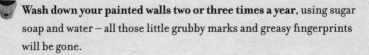 **Wash down your painted walls two or three times a year**, using sugar soap and water – all those little grubby marks and greasy fingerprints will be gone.

 Keep your windows sparkling – it makes a huge difference. Clean with white vinegar and buff with newspaper. Cheaper than Windolene and streak-free.

 Soda crystals dissolved in warm water make a brilliant job of cleaning paintwork around window frames, which can get quite dusty/gunky if you ignore them.

Resand and reseal wooden floors regularly in areas of heavy wear: e.g. kitchens.

Making Stuff for Your House

Basic curtains aren't as impossible as you might imagine: see www.startsewing.co.uk/howtomakecurtains.html for a set of instructions; there are many others also available online.

The web is awash with absolutely genius decorating blogs, which usually offer a combination of things to buy and things to make yourself (if you can't find them, use their search blog to look for 'DIY' or 'projects'). There are some seriously cool decorating ideas on these. Here is a small selection of some of my favourites. They're like porn for middle-aged women:

www.designspongeonline.com
These two are like (not so) mini Bibles – between them they contain a massive amount of information, tips and inspirations. Be sure to check out their archives and shopping guides also.

www.decor8.blogspot.com

http://blogs1.marthastewart.com/blueprint
The blog belonging to the now sadly defunct *Blueprint* magazine. Loads of ingenious, low-cost decorating ideas.

www.dominomag.com/daily/blogs/
dailydose/girl_about_town
Rita Konig's ever-entertaining decorating blog – she's not big on cheapness, but she's always inspiring.

www.apartmenttherapy.com
The daddy of urban home deco sites; wonderful and comprehensive.

What Not to Scrimp On

A comfy mattress: you're going to spend a third of your life lying on it, and a bad mattress (which I'm afraid means a cheap mattress) will make that third uncomfortable and potentially harmful (it may do your back in). Always buy the best mattress you can afford and look after it by turning it regularly.

Don't bother with cheap paint: it doesn't go on evenly, looks rubbish and can deposit nasty chalky marks on your clothes when you brush past a wall. You'll end up needing loads of coats and the finished effect is unlikely to be impressive.

Buy the best boiler you can afford. Boiler problems are unbearable – 7 p.m. on a freezing December night, with no heating and no hot water – and can be extremely costly to fix, plus the emergency plumber you'll need to call out will charge you exorbitantly for the privilege.

I had never been remotely interested in understanding how money works – the word 'money' just made me feel like singing songs from *Cabaret*. I literally knew nothing. FTSE? No idea, sounds like snogging with toes under the table. ISA? Like a Scottish girl's name: Isa and her wee sister Iona. 'The markets'? My favourite is Portobello. People who work in the City? Twats. And so on.

But it eventually dawned on me, aged forty-two and in tentative control of my finances for the first time ever, that you can't exist in the world and live in a capitalist society and know nothing about how money works: it's just wilful stupidity. Yes, I'd rather be reading a book or looking at a picture (or staring into space) than ponder the surprisingly complex question of mortgages, and it's not like I now fall on the financial pages, thrilled to my core and hungry for more knowledge (well, not often). But glazing over any time anyone mentions pensions or exchange rates or monetary policy isn't really that much of a virtue. Ignorance rarely is.

My embryonic interest was really pricked earlier this year by an article by John Lanchester in the *Guardian*. It was ostensibly about the credit crunch and us all sleepwalking head first into recession. It was, amazingly to me, incredibly interesting. Part of this was to do with Lanchester's skill as a writer, but part of it was that the life of money, if you will, had an almost novelistic shape. These incredibly dramatic and exciting things happened to it – and by extension to all of us – and there was passion, fire, spirit, drama, intense dodginess, risk . . . The article was a complete eye-opener.* Skip this chapter if you understand money, but read on if, like me, its ins and outs have always been a complete mystery to you. This is my attempt at explaining how money works, how you can make it work for you and how it's not cool to adopt an ostrich attitude on the grounds that money simply isn't very interesting.

Aside from anything else, it actually *is* interesting. What is perhaps most interesting and strange about it (to me) is that the whole of money – global economies and so on – rests on a single act of faith, which is a collective belief in the value of money. Without that belief, money is meaningless and worthless: it's just bits of paper or metal. You can't eat it, or drink it, and it won't keep you warm at night. You could sit in a house with £10 million in freshly minted notes, but unless you existed in a society that let you swap those notes for *stuff*, you'd starve to death.

Happily (and really rather crazily if you think about it for too long: I mean, people snigger at religious faith, but this is in another league altogether), we do have belief and faith, which means we can use the little bits of paper or metal by exchanging them for things. That's what money basically is: a sophisticated system of IOUs, some of which are instantly redeemable, some of which are redeemable at a later date.

---

* *You can read it here: www.guardian.co.uk/business/2008/mar/22/creditcrunch.*
  marketturmoil.

OK, here beginneth the lesson.* Money is bought and sold (this is where my brain starts exploding, because the more you think about it, the more intensely peculiar it becomes) on markets, like anything else; oddly, money is used to buy money. When you take out a loan, you are effectively buying money, because you have to give back more than you initially borrowed (hence interest rates being so important: they dictate the value of money).

For an economy to be healthy, people need to be spending money, but they also need to be borrowing it. If borrowing money suddenly gets much more expensive (as it is at the time of writing), then it follows that people rein in their spending and economic growth slows down. If economic growth slows down, people start to lose their jobs.

As I understand it (and some pernickety economists might argue with me), recession occurs when the measures of economic activity – employment, investment, corporate profits – decline. It can result in deflation (falling prices) or rapid inflation (rising ones). Rapid inflation is bad news for the economy, because it means money is basically losing its value in terms of the goods it can be exchanged for.

Exchange rates are an interesting component to all of this. The value of the pound also depends on its performance in world markets, as indicated by exchange rates. I never understood this before, but what it means is that the value of the pound is dictated by who wants to buy it (by investing in the UK) and how much they want to buy it for. As with inflation, the whole thing needs to be delicately balanced: if the pound is mighty and super-strong, other currencies become cheaper to buy, as do imported goods – but it becomes harder for British people/companies to sell goods abroad.

* *Thanks to finance wizard Jamie Leitch for making sure I teach this lesson correctly.*

Borrowing Money

Banks make money by lending money at higher interest rates than they borrow it for. They lend money to us, but also to each other: vast sums are constantly being shifted between them. Their godfather is the Bank of England, which is known as the 'lender of last resort' and, if it must, will provide a safety net by being able to bail out banks that get into trouble.

To understand borrowing money, you need to understand about Annual Percentage Rates, or APR. What this represents is the cost of a loan (the interest and all other charges) over its entire term, expressed as an annual percentage. In the UK, all lenders have to tell you what their APR is before you sign an agreement with them. If you're borrowing, the lower the APR, the better the deal. APRs are your friend, so pay attention to them.

Current Accounts

70 per cent of people bank with the UK's Big Four – Lloyds, HSBC, Barclays and NatWest * – because they're the ones we're familiar with and trust. However, their current accounts often give out practically no interest and they may also charge obscenely high interest on overdrafts. Go to www. moneysupermarket.com or www.uswitch.com to check out the alternatives.

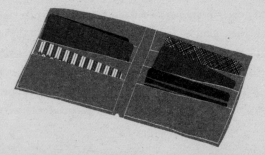

* *According to* Love is Not Enough: A Smart Woman's Guide to Money *by Merryn Somerset Webb (HarperCollins, new ed. 2008)*

Credit Cards

Beware, is my advice. Credit cards offer a useful form of short-term borrowing, but you can get into the most incredible trouble if you are not in a position to repay the whole amount you've borrowed every month. Many companies make a fortune from interest and other charges. The average APR on most credit cards is around a whopping 16 per cent. Unless you pay your debt off each month, you are charged this huge interest rate on the whole amount, *including the amount you've paid off*. It is terrifyingly simple for credit card debts to spiral out of control very quickly. Only use a credit card if you know you can afford the full monthly repayments. That whole 'minimum repayment' malarkey is how people get caught up in circles of debt.

If you are able to pay off your balance in full every month, think about signing up for a cash back credit card. There are all kinds of deals out there – some actually give you money for making purchases and some may give you free travel insurance – check out www.moneysavingexpert.com/cards/cashback-credit-cards.

My other piece of advice is have one or maybe two credit cards (I have one for normal purchases and one for online shopping), and that's it. Too many credit cards make managing your finances – which is hardly a piece of cake in the first place – unnecessarily complicated and challenging (to say nothing of expensive). Never use a credit card at an ATM (cash machine) as it is likely you'll be charged an immediate fee for doing so and interest will start ticking from that point – you may as well amuse yourself by burning fivers.

Balance Transfers

Getting a new credit card when you're struggling to manage your existing ones may sound like a mad idea, but it can make sense and save you money if it involves a credit card balance transfer. What this basically means is that the new credit card company takes over your debts, but often gives you a period of grace in which to sort yourself out. During this period, they charge dramatically lower interest on the transferred balance (2, 1 or even 0 per cent interest is possible). This introductory rate usually lasts between six and twelve months. So that's nice. But look out for hefty transfer fees – some banks charge a percentage of the balance transferred, which can be costly if that balance is high, so make sure there is a cap on the amount.

If you're savvy about it, though, balance transfers can present the solution to spiralling credit card debts, because they allow you to pay off the debt without incurring further charges. You could, in theory, keep doing this – shifting your debt from company to company, being given more and more time to pay it off – but do be careful: it requires major diligence and attention to detail, and those transfer fees are likely to mount up.

Store Cards

These are a bad idea unless you can pay the debt in full each month. They almost always have higher APRs than credit cards. I say, get them for invites to special sales previews, but don't actually use them to buy anything unless you can 100 per cent afford it.

Loans

Loans are for borrowing money in the longer term. There are a number of different costs associated with taking out a loan, such as set-up costs, administration costs, interest and account closure costs. These vary from lender to lender, from loan type to loan type and from loan to loan.

What this slew of charges means is that it is quite hard for the prospective borrower to compare the costs of different loans. Companies often advertise a low interest rate for a loan, giving the impression of a marvellous deal, and yet once all the other costs have been taken into consideration, it can end up costing you much more than a loan at a higher interest rate with lower associated costs.

Our friend the trusty APR allows for direct comparisons (it takes all costs into account). Lenders are required by law to disclose the APR, but it is usually in much smaller print than the interest rate, because it is a less alluring figure.

Secured Loan

This is a loan which is backed by assets belonging to the borrower in order to decrease the risk assumed by the lender. Usually the assets in question are whatever you have borrowed the money to buy – the house, the car, the plasma TV screen, etc. The assets may be forfeited to the lender if the borrower fails to make the necessary payments: i.e. the bailiffs are on their way round . . .

The most common form of secured loan is called a mortgage. Because secured loans are less risky for the lender, they are usually cheaper than unsecured loans. Apart from buying a house, secured loans are mostly suitable for borrowing large amounts of money over the longer term, such as for home improvements or buying a car.

Unsecured Loan

An unsecured loan means the lender relies on your promise to pay it back. They're taking a bigger risk than with a secured loan, so interest rates tend to be higher. You normally have set payments over an agreed period and penalties may apply if you want to repay the loan early.

Unsecured loans are often more expensive and less flexible than secured loans, but suitable if you want a short-term loan (one to five years). Watch out for payment holidays: it may sound great at first to not have to start paying off your loan for the first six months or so but be aware that you'll most likely still be charged interest over these months.

Investing Money

If you've got some spare cash, there are lots of options for investing money, ranging from the very safe to the very high risk. The best advice (unless you enjoy an element of serious risk in your life) is not to put all your eggs in one basket – spread your investment over different companies and different investment schemes.

When you are saving money, it doesn't (alas) sit in a vault in the bank, guarded by goblins; it is being lent to somebody else. Because rates for borrowing money from banks are always higher than savings rates, it is better to pay off outstanding debts before investing your money. Having said that, you should always try to keep a rainy day fund in case of emergencies.

Savings Accounts

Your first port of call should be an ISA (individual savings account). With an ISA you can save up to £7,200 each year and NOT PAY TAX on the income you receive from your investment. Be aware that if you withdraw any money from your ISA, you won't be able to top it up to £7,200 again in that tax year. Individual savers are able to invest in two separate ISAs in any one tax year: one cash ISA and one stocks and shares ISA, but the £7,200 limit is across both ISAs.

If you have further money to invest, other savings accounts offer relatively high rates of interest, dependent on a range of terms and conditions, but (unless you have a very low income) you will be taxed on the income you receive from the investment.

For savings advice, including which banks have the best rates, go to www.moneysavingexpert.com/savings/savings-accounts-best-interest.

Bonds

A bond is a debt security, similar to an IOU. When you purchase a bond, you are lending money to a government, corporation or other entity known as the issuer. In return for the loan, the issuer normally promises to pay you a specified rate of interest during the life of the bond and to repay the face value of the bond (the principal) when it 'matures' or becomes due. UK government bonds are known as gilts and usually have lower interest rates because the risk of default is seen as low. Corporation bonds pay differing amounts of interest depending on what the risk is (how stable the company is perceived to be).

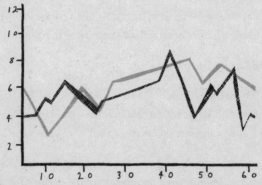

Shares

Shares are different from bonds in that you actually buy yourself ownership of a piece of a company. Shareholders regularly receive payment of dividends that depend on the net profit of the company (and are at the directors' discretion). Generally speaking, shares are riskier investments than bonds, especially in the early stages of a company's life, but remember that bonds are only as stable as the entity you are loaning to.

In the UK shares are bought and sold on the London Stock Exchange (www.londonstockexchange.com). This is essentially a marketplace where people come together to buy and sell shares, all done electronically.

FTSE

The FTSE is basically the name for a set of indices on the London Stock Exchange that show how well a set of company stocks is performing. It gives a sample snapshot of UK-based stocks and an indication as to how they are performing generally.

Here's how the FTSE works (hooray! You too can stop looking completely baffled at the end of *Newsnight*): the 'Index' is how the FTSE is measured and is a running numerical total which can go up and down. In most cases, up is better. The index doesn't actually measure anything in particular – it simply gives a scale against which the values of stock can be measured as going up or down.

A higher total means the value of the market has grown. A lower total means more people have been selling and getting their money out.

Different indices:

FTSE All Share measures how all the companies on the London Stock Exchange are doing. Tracking this index is a good way of measuring a general trend in the market, as it spans all companies and sectors.

FTSE 100 measures the largest 100 companies by value. These businesses make up around 80 per cent of the entire FTSE and thus the FTSE 100 is a good measure of how well big business is doing in the UK.

FTSE 250 measures the next 250 biggest companies based on value. So these two indices (the FTSE 100 and the FTSE 250) incorporate the 350 biggest companies listed in the UK.

There are many major financial markets around the world and many different indices used to assess the performance of the companies listed, but they all work in exactly the same way.

Property

House prices are a huge factor in determining how well an economy is doing. Steadily increasing house prices = healthy economy. However, the more house prices increase, the more money you have to borrow when taking out a mortgage (this is particularly problematic for first-time buyers).

Property value is a largely illusory thing. It's all very well making a profit on the house you are selling, but you still have to buy a new house to move into (which will most likely also have increased in value). Therefore the only way you will ever actually realize the profit you make on a property is if you downsize considerably and move to rural Wales.

Mortgages

Mortgages ought to be straightforward: the idea is you borrow money to buy a house and pay interest on the loan. But, alas, it's not as straightforward as at first appears. Mortgages are a complicated business.

In a hugely competitive market, building societies and banks are continually updating and extending their range of mortgages. The list is extensive and baffling. Essentially what you are doing is taking out a loan based on how much you can afford and on the value of the property, for a length of time agreed between you and the lender. There are two main types of mortgage: repayment or interest-only, and then there are endowment mortgages.

Repayment Mortgages

Each monthly payment pays off a little of the capital, as well as the interest on the loan for that month. By the end of the term, the mortgage is cleared. This is widely considered to be the most easy to understand and least risky type of mortgage.

Interest-Only Mortgages

With this type of mortgage, you pay off the interest on the loan but not the capital itself. At the end of the mortgage term you are expected to repay the capital (how you fund this is your business). These mortgages are therefore a cheaper option.

Endowment Mortgages

An endowment is an insurance policy that pays out a lump sum at the end of a set period or on death, whichever comes first. With an endowment mortgage you use an endowment policy to provide life insurance and save funds to repay the loan at the end of the term (usually between twenty and twenty-five years). If the investment performs badly, you could face a shortfall on your loan at the end of the repayment period. In the 1980s and 1990s endowments were very popular and heavily marketed by lenders when the stock market was high. However, many people were not told of the investment risk and lenders have had to face claims for compensation. As a result, endowment mortgages have declined sharply in popularity. Relatively few endowments are sold today, but there are still millions of policies yet to mature.

The interest you are charged on the mortgage is based on the Bank of England base rate (which is reviewed monthly). You can choose between different deals for your interest rate, such as variable, fixed or discounted.

Variable Rates

This means you pay the going rate on your loan. The mortgage rate either changes every time interest rates change or the overall effect of any interest rate changes is calculated once a year and payments are altered accordingly. Whatever kind of mortgage you start with, it is likely to change to a variable rate at some point.

Fixed Rates

This means the interest rate is fixed for an agreed period – often two to five years. These are ideal for budgeting or if you think rates might increase. You do not benefit if rates fall and will face penalties if you try to quit. Very low rates may tempt you, but they can be used to trap you into paying over the odds at a future date. Check how long you will have to stay with the lender before you can switch without penalty.

Long-term fixed-rate mortgages (up to twenty-five years) are also available. These tie you down for the foreseeable future (a serious amount of commitment is involved), but offer some security amid climbing interest rates and an uncertain financial market.

Capped Rates

These are fixed, but if rates fall you pay the lower rate. Such deals can be good for budgeting.

Discounted Rates

Under this type of mortgage the borrower is offered a discount off the lender's variable rate. The rate paid will fluctuate in line with changes in the variable rate. The discount applies over a set term.

Pensions

And finally pensions. Yes, I know – deeply unsexy. Deeply risky too. I know four people who have dutifully paid into their pension fund for decades on end, only to have it all go tits-up forty years down the line. Personally, I treat my property as my pension. But do pay attention. This is what you need to know:

- **Unless you have a private income or are due to inherit untold riches, you need to sort your pension out now if you want any kind of reasonable quality of life as an old person.** Fact, as David Brent would say. The number of people who have made inadequate or no provision for their retirement is on the up. According to the Association of British Insurers, the nation is saving £27 billion less than it needs to survive in retirement.

- **In order to qualify for a full state pension, you have to work for thirty-nine years (it's changing to thirty years in 2010).** If you are a woman and have taken time out to look after your children, you're unlikely to manage to put in this number of years. Add the fact that lots of women don't usually save money for the future, but rather spend it on family-related needs, and you begin to see how you might have difficulty paying for your eventual (wahey) nursing home.

What to Do

- **Figure out roughly how much you will need when you retire.** What do you see yourself doing? Where will you live? How many cats will you have? Do you see yourself doing lots of travelling?

Go to **www.pensioncalculator.org**, which will help you work out how much you need to save (the general rule is take your age, halve it and save that percentage of your salary every month).

If you haven't got a pension, get one.
See www.pensionsadvisoryservice.org.uk.

Types of Pension

State Pensions

Will you get a state pension? This site tells you the answer, and if yes, how much: www.worksmart.org.uk/money/basic_state_pension.
It's worth noting that your state pension is very unlikely to cover your grand retirement plans, so you might have to make extra provisions.

Company Pensions

These are generally regarded as the best kind, as your employer contributes money to the pension and you can normally transfer your company pension if you change jobs. Just pray your employer doesn't go bust or you'll lose the whole lot, your contributions included.

Personal Pensions

With a personal pension you make your own arrangements with an investment manager and normally save a fixed monthly amount.

Self-Invested Personal Pensions (SIPPs)

With a personal pension, your investment manager chooses where you put your money but with a SIPP, you decide. They range in complexity but the simplest ones can be arranged and managed online.

Personal Finance and Budgeting

The one thing that made more of a difference to me than anything else was sitting down – well, forcing myself to sit down – with a load of bank statements and comparing my income to my expenditure. It helps to keep a diary of what you spend – little things that are easy to dismiss or forget, such as a new eyeshadow or a Frappuccino, all add up in quite a terrifying manner. It is also worth keeping on top of your direct debits and standing orders. I was so scared of opening bank statements for so long that I didn't realize that I was still paying out monthly amounts for services I no longer used, including an Internet service provider I hadn't had any dealings with since 2002. Sitting down and sorting all of this out may not gladden your heart – you will almost inevitably discover that you are spending too much – but there are many ways to cut back on expense, as I hope this book has shown. There are also many ways to cut back on bills: they live at www. moneysavingexpert.com.

Some useful sites:

www.moneysavingexpert.com/banking/budget-planning
A downloadable budget planning spreadsheet and a completely invaluable tool.

www.direct.gov.uk/en/MoneyTaxAndBenefits/index.htm
Government site with helpful information on money, tax and benefits.

www.moneymadeclear.fsa.gov.uk/home.html
The Financial Services Authority (FSA) is an independent body that regulates the financial services industry in the UK and their website provides clear impartial information.

The last thing I will say on this subject is please, please don't stick your head in the sand. It is – I know to my cost – very easy to shove red envelopes in a special place (like under the fridge), unopened and ignored. But there's only ever one loser in these situations and it is you. You lose more and more with every month that passes. Take control. Phoning your credit card company and explaining that you've messed up but want to remedy the situation in whatever way you can manage is a hundred times more likely to succeed than simply pretending the situation doesn't exist in the first place. In my (considerable) experience, people are keen to help you fix things and to come up with a workable repayment plan. Also, by doing this you don't necessarily bugger up your credit history for the foreseeable future. More to the point, you won't wake up in the night from nightmares about debtors' prison. Take responsibility for your finances and no matter how bad or tight things seem now, they will improve immeasurably in the future. Keep ignoring them and the only way is down.

Emotional
Thrift

I believe that part of the reason so many of us feel obscurely dissatisfied in some way is to do with our strange, deluded (and very unthrifty) expectations. I also believe that these are a direct consequence of two things: a) celebrity culture, in which everyone always seems beautiful, rich, happy and fulfilled, and we by comparison seem plain, poor, beset with small miseries and chronically unfulfilled/ frustrated; and b) the sneaky influence, and legacy of, all those thousands of self-help books, which have now been around for a couple of decades and basically all contain the same message: you're super-special and deserve everything, and if you're not getting it, it's because you're a victim.

Point a) is easily dismissed: it's called PR and I sincerely hope that the lovely readers of this book have enough gumption to see the smoke and mirrors for what they are. (It's also called airbrushing, and sometimes eating disorder, and often drug habit.)

Point b) is more prevalent and I think more damaging. You don't even have to have read the self-help books for their message to have trickled through, as though by osmosis. We're all fluent in psychobabble and we all love to emote – both of which aptitudes would have our grandparents spinning in their graves. We seem to have lost any idea of the merits of self-control or even piping down occasionally.

This isn't (quite) a plea for all of our human transactions to have a tragically repressed *Brief Encounter* vibe about them. But it *is* a plea for a return to a stiffening of upper lips. Emoting all over the place is exhausting, makes you vulnerable, and is seldom the cure-all it has been touted as being. If it were, the generations that are fluent in psychobabble wouldn't strike one as being so profoundly emotionally unsatisfied.

We're all damaged to some extent, and we all carry around our stuff, our emotional burdens and our neuroses. They're not that interesting. I liked it better when the answer to 'How are you?' was inevitably, 'Fine, thank you', even if the person in question only had moments to live. Instead, what you now often get in response to your polite but fairly unconcerned enquiry is a detailed catalogue of grievances and perceived injuries, wrongs and slights. But being free with personal information in this way doesn't make you an 'open' or 'emotionally in tune' person. It just makes you sound really needy, like you're the only thing that matters.

Now, it may well be that you genuinely believe you *are* the only thing that matters – many people do, to a lesser or greater extent. But surely you can manage to keep your egomania to yourself? It isn't the most attractive of characteristics, even if it is a very human one – and, to be perfectly frank, nobody cares as much about you as you do. Going on and on about yourself, or about a thing that has happened to you, is incredibly bad manners – it makes any conversational exchange about you and you only. It also marks you out, in my view, as a person who cannot successfully function on his or her own, and constantly needs the praise or interest of other people in order to feel like a functioning human being. This sucks. It is amazingly tiresome to have to deal with and I wish people would desist – not just because it would make me happy, but because I genuinely think it would make them happier too. If you are what you eat, you are also what you think, and if what you think out loud is relentlessly self-centred and negative, it kind of follows that you're unlikely to be especially chipper.

The fact of the matter is, bad things happen all the time, to all of us. They're just bad things. They don't make us victims unless we want to be. What you need to do with a bad thing is get over it, not worry about it or examine it from every angle and share all your insights with anyone who cares to listen. Your boyfriend has dumped you: it's very sad, but there you go. It doesn't get any less sad if you discuss it solidly for three weeks (or three months) and turn every single conversation round to the subject of your deep and unique unhappiness. A loved one is ill: it's grim, but it happens. Speak to people in a similar boat if you think that might comfort you, but, again, don't bring every innocuous chat round to the subject of adult incontinence pants; it's not cheering anyone up, least of all yourself. Be adult: shoulder your burden, process it and move on. Children blab and wail, but you're not a child. Don't be emotionally incontinent.

Be realistic with your expectations. I mean, I'd really like to cuddle a unicorn, but it ain't going to happen. Know yourself and aim for the aimable, not for the completely out-there: you'll save yourself quantities of disappointment. We'd all like to marry incredibly studly millionaires with PhDs and well-developed social consciences, but I suspect they're probably a bit thin on the ground. We'd all like to be promoted into the stratosphere, but it's unlikely to happen if we insist on leaving at 5.30 on the dot and are intent on our 'right' to every single holiday. And anyway, sometimes what you have under your nose is exactly right for you, even if it (or he) doesn't quite match up to the fantasy version. Fantasies are just that: imaginary. It seems to me that too many of us believe so much in fantasies that we waste all the goodness of what is real and tangible.

Appreciate what you've got, even the really small things. For me, those really small things are often domestic, and I hope this book has communicated my enthusiasm for the nourishing significance of the very small. Everyday happiness, as opposed to one-off great bursts of pure ecstasy, is intricately tied in with tiny everyday events: the jaunty-looking teapot that pours without dribbling, the children's bathtime, blossom in spring, an especially good book. These things aren't sexy, or glamorous, or envy-making, but they are the fabric of all our days. Concentrating on them, and on all the small joys they provide, can be intensely fulfilling. Moaning because you can't afford a £300 pair of shoes is not. Neither is moaning *tout court*.

Be happy. We are all blessed, in thousands of different ways. So we're not a size 6, cavorting on a yacht with George Clooney. So what? I'd rather be sniffing my babies' heads. There is enormous beauty in everyday life, and it doesn't cost any money to look at it and feel glad to be alive.

Index